The TRADITIONAL Shops & Restaurants of LONDON

A Guide to Century-Old Establishments and New Classics

EUGENIA BELL

Photographs by Phil Nicholls

THE LITTLE BOOKROOM

NEW YORK

© 2007 Eugenia Bell

Photographs © 2007 Phil Nicholls

Design Louise Fili Ltd

Library of Congress Cataloging-in-Publication Data

Bell, Eugenia.

The traditional shops and restaurants of London :

a guide to century-old establishments and new classics / by Eugenia Bell.

p. cm.

Includes bibliographical references and index.

ISBN–13: 978-1-892145-46-8 (alk. paper)

ISBN–10: 1-892145-46-4 (alk. paper)

1. London (England)—Guidebooks. I. Title.

DA679.B33 2007

381'.109421—dc22   2006037223

The Little Bookroom

1755 Broadway, 5th floor

New York NY 10019

(212) 757-8070

www.littlebookroom.com

Printed in China

Contents

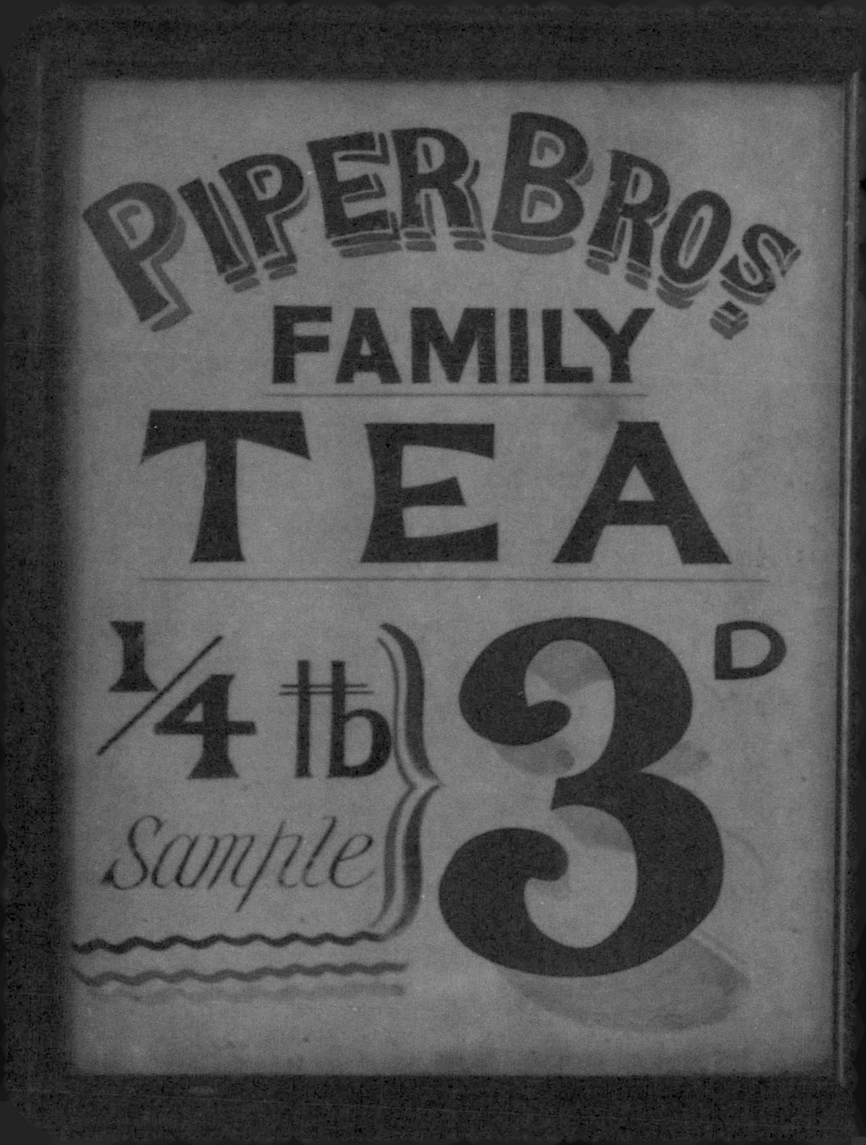
PIPER BROS
FAMILY
TEA
1/4 lb
Sample
3D

Introduction

I moved to London in 2003, and soon discovered that one of the great pleasures of living there is the city's profusion of small-scale, independently owned, and historically significant restaurants, pubs, and shops. In the middle of one of the densest, most diverse boroughs of London, I found a century old flower market, a shop that sold English gardening tools and old Penguin paperbacks, another that sold food only from the British Isles, a small working "city farm" that sold fresh eggs from the hens it raised, and even a former Welsh dairy offering farmhouse cheeses and organic fruit. All of this was virtually at my doorstep.

The newspapers and the BBC every day reported the increasing prevalence (and profits) of large supermarkets and retail chain stores, evidence that British teenagers no longer knew a leek from a lettuce, and reports decried the decline of nearly all that makes Britain British. But the more time I spent in London, and the more I wandered from Bethnal Green to World's End, Muswell Hill to Deptford, the more optimistic I became. Napoleon may never have called Britain a "nation of shopkeepers," as is so often claimed, but London in the new millennium is truly a city of robust shopkeepers and dynamic restaurateurs who are recapturing a sense of the traditional spirit that makes London so unique. And it's that spirit I wanted to capture in this guide.

British consumer society has its origins in the mid- to late seventeenth century, but much of what makes London shops and restaurants memorable is a product of the excesses of the Victorian Age. Britain's colonial expansion of the time meant the introduction of "exotic" goods at prices that made them accessible to vast numbers of people. Meanwhile the advancements of the Industrial Revolution yielded a steady supply of new goods, and a culture of shopping began to evolve. Finally the sheer size of the growing metropolis, then home to nearly 3 million people, ensured a need for multiple specialty shops: Twenty years into Queen Victoria's reign, a London guidebook estimated the city had 23,000 tailors and 40,000 milliners. While not quite in such numbers, the actual and spiritual descendants of many of those specialty shops survive today.

But London has fewer old establishments than one might imagine. Much of the city and its visible history were destroyed by the Great Fire of 1666 and again by German bombing during the Second World War three centuries later. In the decades after the war, it wasn't just the cityscape that was altered: The very fabric of civic life changed as supermarkets replaced local greengrocers, cars and suburbs sounded the death knell for pedestrianized High Streets and with them their local shops, and the sense of village life itself so long enjoyed in London began to disappear. At the time, convenience was viewed as the paramount virtue, decentralized shopping districts were championed, and the local character of neighborhoods was ironed out.

It's not only age that distinguishes some of the best London establishments. London has century-old shops and restaurants, of course—picturesque places that evoke the days when London was shrouded by steam and fog. Too many of them, though, rest on the simple fact of their having survived through the decades and centuries, and they tend to cater explicitly to the tourist trade. I've made a real attempt here to include establishments that celebrate their history less for the tourists it may attract and more for the sheer pleasure of making and selling things in traditional ways. In keeping with the "historical" mission of this guide, it goes without saying why the 300-year-old Twining's tea shop (still family-owned, see page 92) or some older establishments recognized by the royal family (see "The Royal Warrant", page 205) are included. But the "traditional" is slightly more ephemeral and particular. In addition to what might be considered traditional trades (cheese making and hat fitting, for example), I've included shops and eateries—some open less than a decade—that stave off the pressures of conforming to certain expectations of modern shopkeeping and those that have resisted obsolescence and the lures of "convenience" shopping. At some shops you'll have to wait while your purchases are meticulously wrapped (Tracey Neuls, page 73), or indeed at others you may even have to wait while they're being made, as in the case of Mayfair shirt makers or the custom bicycle shop, Witcomb Cycles (page 201).

The shops and eateries in this book all attest to the growing desire for alternatives to the often anonymous pursuits that eating and shopping have become—and without the treacly aftertaste of forlorn nostalgia. They range from pubs opened in the seventeenth century (The Lamb, page 261) to retail shops opened in the twenty-first (Labour and Wait, page 112). But all of them embrace London's history and evince a strong sense of tradition—either their own or that of their adopted neighborhoods. Younger establishments, especially those marked as "New Classics," may not yet have stood the test of time, but they too uphold the

9

ideals of traditional shopkeeping by preserving historic shop fronts or by promoting British products, ingredients, or preparation.

The diversity and depth of the types of shops in London is hardly surprising: This is a city, after all, that had a shop specializing in "smooth pointed combs" and razor straps as early as 1730 (Floris, page 41, which today sells a remarkable range of fine fragrances). But the prevalence of historic restaurants may be more of a surprise. Somerset Maugham once wrote that to eat well in England one should have breakfast three times a day. While I might not mind that at all—the full English breakfast is a sight, if not always a meal, to behold—his implicit criticism of English cuisine no longer holds. There is no longer any reason to fear that one will eat badly in London. The enormous influx of immigrants—from the West Indies, Bangladesh, East Africa, Poland, and elsewhere—has added virtually every cuisine to the city's restaurant map. More to the point of this guide, top London chefs and lesser-known upstarts have vigorously sought to recapture and refresh British cuisine. Most restaurants listed here are devoted to organic, sustainable, and local food sources, and virtually all of them champion eating to take advantage of the best available produce, meat, and fish.

Today it seems as if those who scoffed at the "relics" of retail shops and restaurants increasingly long to bring them back, to restore a sense of traditional London life. Shopping and eating with a historical or traditional focus in mind means seeing a city in the context of its architecture and its social history. It means resisting the kind of obsolescence forecast during the Thatcher era and recapturing some distinctive local texture. It also means supporting independent and family run businesses and helping maintain traditional trades and practices increasingly lost to "modernization" and technology. Crucially, it also means experiencing London more slowly and fully. Rather than the broad overview one might get from taking the Tube to the heights of the London Eye, may I suggest hitting the pavement and walking through London's disappearing "villages" and discovering the city at a slower, perhaps more traditional, pace?

EUGENIA BELL
London, November 2006

A NOTE ABOUT SYMBOLS

♛ represents the number of Royal Warrants a shop or restaurant
has been granted (see page 205 for a full explanation)

🦁 denotes a shop or restaurant considered a New Classic

ART SUPPLY SHOPS

Green & Stone

EST. 1927

259 KING'S ROAD, SW3

☎ 020 7352 0837   ⊖ SLOANE SQUARE

www.greenandstone.com

MONDAY TO SATURDAY 10AM TO 6PM; SUNDAY NOON TO 5PM

AMID THE PENCILS, PASTELS, AND PIGMENTS OF THIS RENOWNED CHELSEA ART SUPPLY STORE IS A WELL-curated selection of antiques ranging from fine old china and etched crystal glasses to drawing compasses, bone rulers, and water-coloring kits in elaborate boxes. The marriage of historical curiosities and artists' supplies suits the shop's hushed, pleasantly cluttered space.

The shop began as a framing service and small supplier of artists' materials inside the Chelsea gallery run by painter Augustus John. Still well-regarded for its framing, it is now one of the oldest art supply stores in London and is indeed one of the oldest shops on the King's Road; it has been in its current location since 1934. It was run by Alfred Green and his son until 1978, when it was taken over by an employee, Rodney Baldwin, who seems to have changed the atmosphere of the shop as little as possible. Productive sounds from the workshop downstairs echo throughout the store. In addition to pigments, brushes, and easels, Green and Stone sells a selection of handsome wood *porte carton*s, mahogany or tiny brass display easels, and their own brand of canvas and leather portfolios.

L. Cornelissen

EST. 1855

105 GREAT RUSSELL STREET, WC1

☎ 020 7636 1045 ⊖ TOTTENHAM COURT ROAD

www.cornelissen.com

MONDAY TO FRIDAY 9:30AM TO 5:30PM; SATURDAY 9AM TO 5PM;

CLOSED SUNDAY

ESTABLISHED IN 1855, CORNELISSEN IS RENOWNED FOR ITS ARTISTS' MATERIALS, PIGMENTS, AND PASTELS. THE shop was originally on Great Queen Street in nearby Covent Garden and moved here in 1987. But the bright green façade is just about the only thing that's new: all the oak fixtures are the originals from the previous site. Sable brushes, tubes of oil, and glass bottles of turpentine are lined up in glass-fronted cabinets as dainty and ordered as a pharmacist's shop.

BOOKSELLERS & MAP SHOPS

Daunt Books

EST. 1990 🦁

83/84 MARYLEBONE HIGH STREET, W1

☎ 020 7724 2295 ⊖ BAKER STREET

www.dauntbooks.co.uk

MONDAY TO SATURDAY 9AM TO 7:30PM; SUNDAY 11AM TO 6PM

CHARMING MARYLEBONE WAS ONCE A RURAL IDYLL, WHERE WINDING LANES WERE BUILT THROUGH FIELDS linking Oxford Street with Regent's Park (Marylebone Lane still follows its original route along the Tyburn brook; see Paul Rothe & Son, page 167, and Tracey Neuls, page 73) before the eighteenth century, when the area became urbanized and fashionable. Its name, the pronunciation of

which is often cause for argument (most people say "mare-luh-bun") is for St. Mary-le-Bourne, the parish church that was the site of the marriage ceremony in Hogarth's *A Rake's Progress*. (Alas it is no longer there; the church that stands on the site now was built beginning in 1817.) In about 1900, the area was replanned, with mansion blocks and townhouses and a High Street. A residential feel still exists today. For much of the twentieth century,

Marylebone's reputation was one of wealth, plastic surgery, and blue hair rinse. Around 1999, the High Street was redeveloped and "rebranded," and the newly polished product—a villagey shopping street away from the nearby mania of Oxford Street—is one of upscale clothing chains, gastropubs, a Conran shop, and foodie palaces. And, in fact, it is one of the most pleasant shopping streets in central London. Much of the late Victorian and Edwardian retail architecture is still visible, but it is probably no better illustrated and preserved than at Daunt Books.

The shop was established in 1990 by a former banker named James Daunt in a three-storey, skylit space that was designed as a bookshop in the early 1910s. The original galleries in the right-hand room remain, as do the oak staircase and stained-glass skylight. The fine right-hand frontage of the store is original; the left-hand side was carved to match in the 1990s. Inside is a dream bookshop: well-stocked, always busy, but

somehow never crowded, and staffed with helpful booksellers who nevertheless always let customers browse to their heart's content. It has an unusual shelving system: Books in the skylit room are arranged by country regardless of whether they are fiction, travel writing, reference, cookery, or travel guides.

(Note that Daunt now has branch shops in Hampstead, Belsize Park, and Holland Park.)

Foyles

EST. 1906

113-119 CHARING CROSS ROAD, WC2

☎ 020 7437 5660   ⊖ TOTTENHAM COURT ROAD

www.foyles.co.uk

MONDAY TO SATURDAY 9:30AM TO 9PM; SUNDAY NOON TO 6PM

THE ORIGIN OF FOYLES READS LIKE THE PREMISE FOR A VINTAGE EALING STUDIOS COMEDY: AT THE TURN OF THE twentieth century, two brothers fail their civil service exams and place an ad to sell their textbooks. The response is so overwhelming that they decide that selling textbooks is a smart career move, and in 1906 they open a bookstore specializing in textbooks, in Charing Cross Road, the heart of what was becoming London's Bookseller's Row.

A century later, William and Gilbert Foyle's modest textbook enterprise has evolved into what is arguably London's best independent bookstore, and certainly its largest. Over five floors, you can buy an enormous range of books, magazines, and sheet music. There is also a huge children's book department with a fish tank that is home to a piranha, an impressive jazz record shop

upstairs, and a lovely café.

The store recently underwent a massive refurbishment that, to the dismay of some regular customers, has done away with its eclectic shelving system. But if things are more orderly around Foyles these days, customers may find some consolation in other, happier, changes. The family-owned shop hosts an impressive roster of events and has opened smaller concessions (featuring site-appropriate history and guide books) in some of London's historic spots, including the Tower of London, Banqueting House, and Kensington Palace.

G. Heywood Hill Ltd.

EST. 1936

10 CURZON STREET, W1

☎ 020 7629 0647   ⊖ GREEN PARK

www.heywoodhill.com

MONDAY TO FRIDAY 9AM TO 5:30PM; SATURDAY 9AM TO

12:30PM; CLOSED SUNDAY

HEYWOOD HILL AND HIS WIFE, ANNE, OPENED THIS INCON-SPICUOUS MAYFAIR BOOKSHOP—TRY TO FIND THE SIGN signaling the entrance!—in 1936. In 1943, Heywood Hill went to serve in the army and handed the reins to employee Nancy Mitford. After Heywood returned to shopkeeping, Mitford, who had held a financial stake in the store, sold her share back to Hill in 1948 saying, "Doing business with friends is impossible...Do let's have a divorce."

A charming history of the shop can be found in *The Bookshop at 10 Curzon Street*, a collection of letters between Mitford and Hill (edited by the present proprietor John Saumarez-Smith and revealing Mitford's deep dedication to the shop and to its revolving cast of customers) and in Heywood Hill's own *A Bookseller's War*, which contains the moving letters

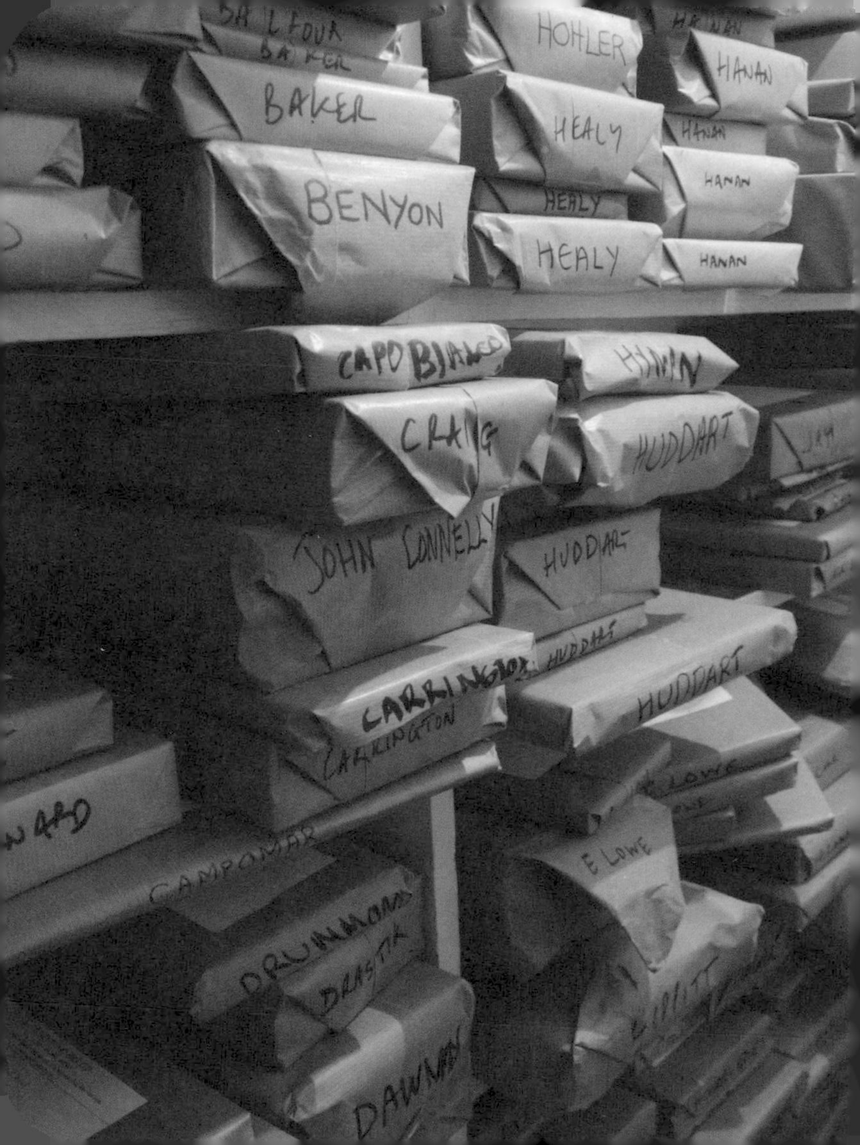

written to his wife while he was in the army. Since the 1970s, Saumarez-Smith has run the shop with the same sense of understated gentility that has always characterized the shop. If Anthony Powell and Evelyn Waugh no longer frequent the bookstore, their spirit certainly haunts it.

The shop sits across the street from the entrance to Shepherd Market, which looks like a quaint tangle of small streets. The Market was anything but quaint when builder and entrepreneur Edward Shepherd laid it out in 1735 on the site of the two-week-long May Fair (which gave the area its name). While Shepherd's shops and houses were a popular destination for the servants of Mayfair's grand homes, it always had something of the louche about it, and still does. The area was portrayed in Patrick Hamilton's 1929 novel *The Midnight Bell* as a hive of prostitution. Though the tangly alleyways remain, the storefronts have almost all been given over to run-of-the-mill sandwich shops, dry cleaners, and off-licenses. In any case, it is still worth a stroll through Shepherd Market for atmosphere and a pint at the Victorian Ye Grapes pub.

Hatchards

EST. 1797 ♛♛♛

187 PICCADILLY, W1

☎ 020 7439 9921   ⊖ PICCADILLY CIRCUS

www.hatchards.co.uk

MONDAY TO SATURDAY 9:30AM TO 7PM; SUNDAY NOON TO 6PM

IN THE EIGHTEENTH CENTURY, BOOKSELLING IN LONDON WAS CONCENTRATED IN THE STRAND—"A VERITABLE HIGHway of books"—where it had moved from near St. Paul's and Holborn. Booksellers were beginning to distance themselves from the mechanical trade of book making at this time, but continued to publish books and sell them in premises which also acted as de facto social clubs for those politically disinclined or socially unable to join the elite clubs of the time. (The Royal Horticultural Society was established at Hatchards in 1804.)

In the late eighteenth century, John Hatchard started off as an apprentice to a London printer, for whom he worked for less than a month. Wanting to enter the book trade in some capacity, he apprenticed to a bookseller/publisher in 1782, and then joined the firm of a well-known bookseller, Thomas Payne, near where the National Gallery stands today. He quit in 1797 to open his own bookshop in Piccadilly, when it was still a suburb and few other shops had yet emerged to serve the higher classes ensconced around St. James's and Pall Mall.

Hatchard's first activity was to publish a pamphlet critical of the

French Revolution. He called it the foundation of his fortunes; Hatchard's was a success and soon became the chief haunt of the Tories. In 1817, the shop moved to its present premises, where the Duke of Wellingon is said to have come on horseback to make his purchases. Over the ensuing century, successive Hatchard family members took over the business. In 1891, manager Edwin Shepherd bought it with the help of a previous manager named Alfred Taylor.

An early description of the bookshop described "heaps of narrow staircases, dark corners, and low-ceilinged attics all fitted with books. An atmosphere rather sombre and religious hung over the whole place." The atmosphere at Hatchards today is little changed, though the shop is a bit more orderly, and it retains the character and customer service that is the hallmark of this rightfully famous and respected shop.

John Sandoe Books

EST. 1957 🦁

10 BLACKLANDS TERRACE, SW4

☎ 020 7589 9473 ● SLOANE SQUARE

www.johnsandoe.com

MONDAY, TUESDAY, THURSDAY, FRIDAY 9:30AM TO 5:30PM;
WEDNESDAY 9:30AM TO 7:30PM; SATURDAY 9:30AM TO 5:30PM;
SUNDAY NOON TO 6PM

THE KING'S ROAD IS CHELSEA'S MAIN THOROUGHFARE, THE BACKBONE OF SWINGING SIXTIES LONDON. BIBA, VIVIENNE Westwood (see page 80), and the habitués of the Chelsea Potter pub gave it a glamorous reputation it has long since dispensed with. Today it is a bland expanse of shops aimed at Chelsea's privileged teenagers and

home-decorating obsessives. Small wonder, then, that the long-standing independent John Sandoe Books continues to thrive just a block away. Or perhaps that's exactly why it does: Sandoe's is not like other bookshops.

Behind its squat eighteenth-century façade, tables are piled dangerously high with books. There is hardly a shelving system, though staff claim it just takes time in the shop to decipher it. Perhaps they're right. Somehow, 100,000 titles are packed into the shop. Near the entrance is new inventory and art and architecture books are stacked and shelved in the room to the left. There are two more levels—children's books downstairs, a variety of fiction and non-fiction upstairs—the staircases to which are incredibly steep and narrow. The store does a roaring mail-order trade and is happy to order books it doesn't stock, but the owners make a point of carrying unusual books and catering to those customers who support the store. John Sandoe retired in 1989, when he sold the shop to a staff member and two partners (one a longtime customer). Employees are said to stick around for years (one of them was renowned cookbook writer Elizabeth David's sister; today a marine biologist is on staff), a good thing given the shop's idiosyncrasies!

Samuel French

EST. 1830

52 FITZROY STREET, W1

☎ 020 7255 4300   ⊖ WARREN STREET

www.sameulfrench-london.co.uk

MONDAY TO FRIDAY 9:30AM TO 5:30PM;

SATURDAY 11AM TO 5PM; CLOSED SUNDAY

IN 1843, AN ACT OF PARLIAMENT WAS PASSED THAT BROKE THE PROFESSIONAL THEATER MONOPOLY IN BRITAIN AND allowed a wider range of theaters to stage published plays. The act resulted in audiences being exposed to a wider range of plays than before, and to lesser known drama and new theaters.

The actor and stage manager Thomas Lacy had already been publishing plays for more than a decade at this point—many bought from defunct publishers. His business in the Strand, established in 1830, at the heart of the theater district at the time, began to thrive, and he soon took on a New York-based agent, Samuel French, to represent the plays he published in America. French relocated to London in 1872 and took over the business on Lacy's death in 1874.

It was Samuel French who originated the concept of a publisher controlling performance rights of a play and collecting a royalty on each. In the late nineteenth century, it is said that every major British playwright was represented by French.

Descendents of the Hogg family ran the business until 1975 in premises on Covent Garden's Southampton Row. In 1983, the shop moved to a commanding corner storefront among the sedate Georgian streets of Fitzrovia. The roomy and buzzy shop is a must for any theater enthusiast or student. In addition to play scripts, the shop carries technical books, biographies, Samuel French-published audition and amateur texts and more than 1,500 official acting texts.

The Map House

EST. 1907

54 BEAUCHAMP PLACE, SW3

☎ 020 7589 4325   ⊖ KNIGHTSBRIDGE

www.themaphouse.com

MONDAY TO FRIDAY 10AM TO 6PM; SATURDAY 10AM TO 5PM;
CLOSED SUNDAY

BEAUCHAMP PLACE IS A POSH LITTLE LANE THAT TURNS INTO PONT STREET AND CONNECTS KNIGHTSBRIDGE TO Chelsea's Sloane Street. The typical shop along here reflects the patrician tastes and buying power of the locals, but The Map House stands apart from the endless parade of restaurants and boutiques. Founded in 1907, The Map House has long been a mecca for map lovers and collectors; it may be the most famous map shop in the world.

The shop contains six galleries of maps, prints, and globes. In the front, the Engravings Gallery, contains alphabetized bins and racks holding inexpensive maps of the Americas, botanical prints, and architectural drawings. In the World Gallery, there is a wide collection of British colonial maps of America. The Mews Room and a regally paneled private room hold globes and maps of great value for private viewing only. Original maps by Mercator and rare incunables that record the world before Columbus are sometimes in stock, as are eighteenth-century globes and mechanized tellurians. Fine reproductions and engraved maps and prints start at about £30.

CHEMISTS, PERFUMERIES & SHAVING ACCESSORIES SHOPS

D.R. Harris

EST. 1790 ♛

29 ST. JAMES'S STREET, SW1

☎ 020 7930 3915   ☻ GREEN PARK

www.drharris.co.uk

MONDAY TO FRIDAY 8:30AM TO 6PM; SATURDAY 9:30AM TO 5PM;

CLOSED SUNDAY

D.R. HARRIS HAS BEEN LOCATED IN ST. JAMES'S SINCE 1790, PROVIDING HERBAL REMEDIES, ACCESSORIES, AND SOAPS from four different addresses before settling in at number 29 in 1963. The store has the quiet calm of many establishments in this neighborhood of gentlemanly member's clubs: discreet, courteous, hushed. D. R. Harris has created herbal concoctions to treat the ills of the area's residents since it opened. All of its products are made in England using original recipes and preparations, and the elegantly designed packaging—glass bottles, tubes, soap boxes—was made on the premises until the late 1980s. Products are still displayed in original mahogany cabinets specially made for the previous premises.

The shop features its own Arlington range of shaving creams and soaps, Bay Rum aftershave, and their famous cucumber-based Crystal Eye Gel. There is also small apothecary in the back of the store. Customers can also buy a "pick-me-up"—a noted hangover tonic—for £1 at the counter.

Floris

EST. 1730 ♛♛

89 JERMYN STREET, SW1

☎ 0845 702 3239   ⊖ GREEN PARK

www.florislondon.com

MONDAY TO FRIDAY 9:30AM TO 6PM; SATURDAY 10AM TO 6PM;

CLOSED SUNDAY

FOUNDER JUAN FAMENIAS FLORIS, A NATIVE OF MENORCA, WAS A BARBER AND COMB-MAKER BY TRADE. IN 1730, SOON after his arrival in London, he began blending and selling scents—a skill picked up in Montpellier. The bespoke fragrances took off among Mayfair's fashionable set, and Floris let grooming fall by the wayside. His Jermyn Street premises were transformed into an elegant fragrance boutique with a sideline in the stuff of Victorian necessity: handmade brushes and hatpins. Floris products were hand-mixed and -packaged in the shop's cellar until the 1960s (they are now manufactured in Devon), and sixteen Royal Warrants later, the firm is still family-owned.

The elegant shop, fitted out with Spanish mahogany display cases purchased at the 1851 Great Exhibition, feels like an art gallery. Change is still delivered to the customer on a velvet and mahogany plate, a practice dating to Victorian times when handling money was thought to be unsanitary. The back room of the shop serves as a sort of museum, with antique glass bottles of some of the earlier scents on display.

Geo. F. Trumper
Curzon Street
Mayfair

George F. Trumper

EST. 1875

9 CURZON STREET

☎ 020 7499 1850　⊖　GREEN PARK

www.trumpers.com

MONDAY TO FRIDAY 9AM TO 5:30PM; SATURDAY 9AM TO 1:00PM;

CLOSED SUNDAY

ON A RECENT AFTERNOON, TRUMPER WAS A HIVE OF ACT-IVITY. CUSTOMERS WERE TWO-DEEP AT THE COUNTER browsing razors, asking advice on shaving brushes, stocking up on grooming supplies, and checking in for shaving appointments in the back. All the while, the small professional staff behaved as if the crush was nothing out of the ordinary.

The mahogany shop fittings are stocked with badger-hair shaving soap brushes (the best bristle for a good lather; the handmade ones, which can last up to eight years, cost extra) and their classic Warwick razors come with handles of chrome, faux-tortoiseshell, or gold plate. In the rear of the store are private, mahogany-lined booths for grooming services ranging from haircuts and shaves with hot towels to moustache curling. In addition to supplying myriad shaving accessories and services, Trumper also offers a one-on-one tutorial on the use of traditional open (or straight) razors.

WEST END

Hairdressers

Stylists

GENTS

HAIRCUTTING

Number One Telegraph Street

EST. 1909

1A TELEGRAPH STREET, EC2

⊖ BANK

MONDAY TO FRIDAY 8AM TO 5PM;

CLOSED SATURDAY AND SUNDAY

A DEVELOPED AND OWNED BY THE NEARBY DRAPERS GUILD IN THE LATE 1800S, ALLEY-LIKE TELEGRAPH STREET eventually became home to telegraph companies and stockbrokers. When approaching the red brick No.1 from Moorgate, the barbershop might be easily missed if not for the hand-painted metal sign on the corner in front of the deli advertising "Gents Haircutting." Look for the rickety staircase, lined with silvering mirrored advertisements, follow the slightly damp smell of towels, and descend into an nearly-untouched 1930s set: four original, red leather barber chairs (just a touch worse for wear); an oak panelled and etched-glass cashier's booth; and a railway carriage-style rack for coats

and hats.

Not far from the shop, in Monkwell Square, is the "Barber-Surgeon's Hall" of The Worshipful Company of Barbers, one of London's oldest livery companies, founded in 1308. A Holbein painting hangs inside one of the hall's great rooms. It depicts Henry VIII, his Serjeant-Surgeon, Thomas Vicary, and other medical men and barbers, on the day in 1540 when the king merged the Barbers and the Surgeons guilds.

However, we can be thankful that the two guilds acted somewhat distinctly: barbers displayed blue and white poles, and with the exception of teeth-pulling and bloodletting, were not allowed to perform surgery; surgeons, who displayed red and white-striped poles, were not allowed to cut or shave hair. It was only in 1745 that George II passed several acts to separate surgeons from barbers.

The original owner of the shop retired at 87 in 1970, when Cypriot-born Mr. Kyriacou took over the place. While Mr. Kyriacou, like most barbers, displays red and white stripes, No. 1 is popular among City workers (and a line often forms at the lunch hour) for Kyriacou's £14 haircuts and £15 wet shaves.

Taylor of Old Bond Street

EST. 1854

74 JERMYN STREET, SW1

☎ 020 7930 5544   ⊖ GREEN PARK

www.tayloroldbondst.co.uk

MONDAY TO FRIDAY 9AM TO 6PM; SATURDAY 9AM TO 6PM;

CLOSED SUNDAY

THE DISPLAY WINDOW IS OVERWHELMING: WHO WOULD GUESS THERE WERE SO MANY GROOMING ACCOUTREMENTS for men? Jeremiah Taylor started business in 1854 making hair and scalp tonics from herbal extracts; today, his great-grandson chairs the company that still uses Jeremiah's recipes. Taylor's own brand of shaving soaps and aftershaves, shampoos, and skin creams is handsomely packaged (in boxes and bottles declaring that the firm was "established in the reign of Queen Victoria"). The firm manufactures its goods using only natural ingredients, and its classic Eton aftershave makes one smell like "a clean old grandfather," in the words of one shaving afficionado and fan of Taylor's products. Badger-hair shaving brushes are lined up regimentally beside pewter-backed clothes brushes, and men's and ladies' wooden-handled hairbrushes.

CLOTHIERS, HATTERS & SHOEMAKERS

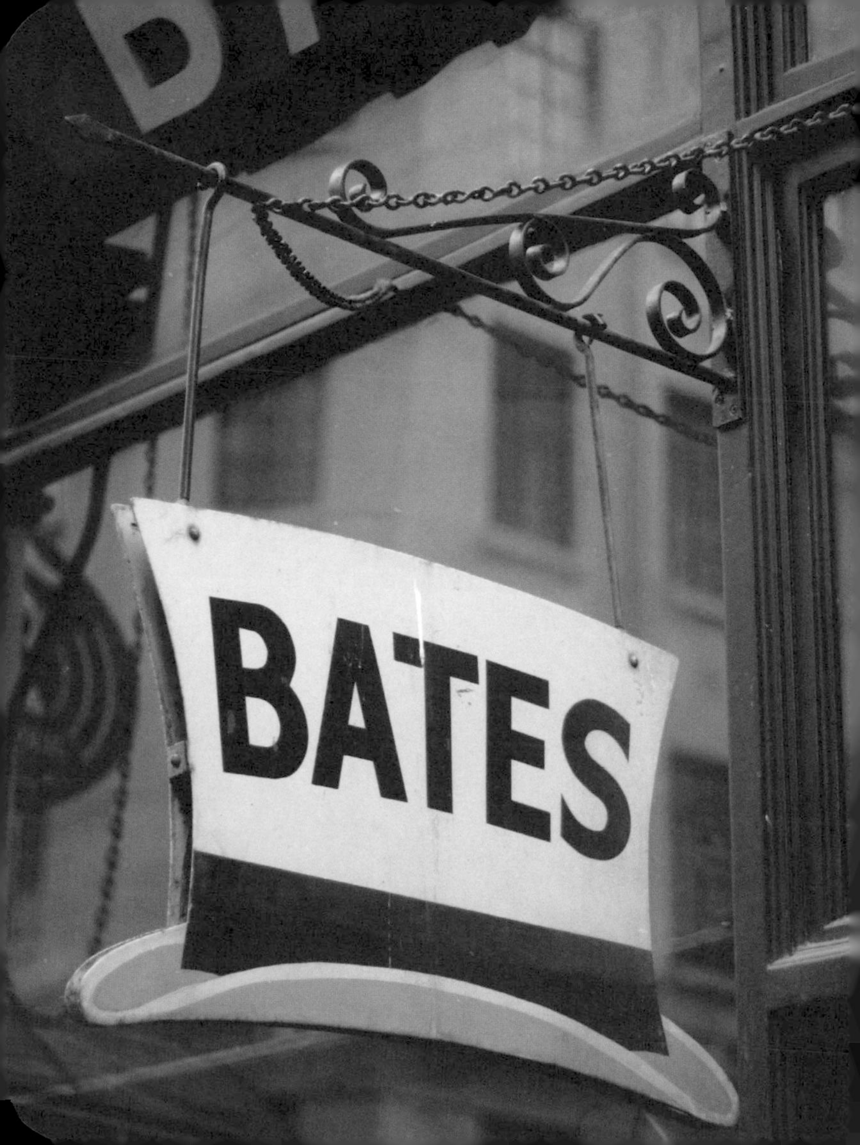
BATES

Bates the Hatter

EST. 1902

21A JERMYN STREET, SW1

☎ 020 7734 2722   ⊖ PICCADILLY CIRCUS

www.bates-hats.co.uk

MONDAY TO FRIDAY 9AM TO 5PM; SATURDAY 9:30AM TO 1PM
AND 2 TO 4PM; CLOSED SUNDAY

FOUNDED IN 1902 JUST DOWN THE BLOCK, THE CURRENT SHOP—NOTABLE FOR ITS SIGN IN THE SHAPE OF A TOP hat—dates from the 1920s, when the owners carved it out of the lobby of the hotel next door. Today, Bates is owned by Timothy Boucher, a friend of the Bates family, to whom the business was left. Unlike Lock and Co. down the street, Bates does not make or fit hats (with the exception of top hats) but sells a huge variety of tweed caps, Panama hats, and formal hats "off the peg" and at reasonable prices. A little dusty and a lot worn, the long narrow shop, however, is no less characterful, if a tad more eccentric, than its neighbor. The shop's orange tabby was a stray that wandered in eighty years ago and hasn't left yet. During the Second World War, Bates produced trench coats and hats for the military in a basement workshop. The shop feels unchanged since.

Ede and Ravenscroft

EST. 1689 ♕ ♕ ♕

93 CHANCERY LANE, WC2

☎ 020 7405 3906 ⊖ CHANCERY LANE

www.edeandravenscroft.co.uk

MONDAY TO FRIDAY 9AM TO 6PM; SATURDAY 10AM TO 3PM;

CLOSED SUNDAY

EDE AND RAVENSCROFT, WHILE HAVING THE DISTINCTION OF BEING LONDON'S OLDEST TAILOR, IS MORE INTEREST-ing for its vital role in the life of those in the legal profession: they have been making robes since their inception, and remain one of a few select tailors who specialize in legal dress. The robes worn by judges in England are almost unchanged since the early 1400s, when judges in London's Middle Temple law courts wore colorful tunics to differentiate them-selves during legal proceedings. When lawyers were inducted into the bar in an investiture ceremony, the Lord Chief Justice would lecture on the importance of donning legal costume. Among other things, it was held that the robes reminded the wearer (and alerted the public) of his profession and that they promoted gravitas and protocol in the profes-sion. In the fifteenth century judges wore scarlet robes (fur lined in the winter). As the dye would have been quite costly at the time, they were most likely reserved for "Red Letter Days" (saints' days or a sovereign's birthday). More typically judges wore green in the summer and violet in winter until it was deemed that somber colors were more appropriate, and duly introduced in the late fifteenth century. More colorful, ceremonial dress is still occasionally worn today for the State Opening of Parliament, for example, or the first day of Michaelmas term (the start of the legal year) or the Queen's birthday.

In addition to its robemaking, Ede and Ravenscroft is one of the last makers and suppliers of the wigs worn by barristers and judges in court. Wigs were originally worn as a fashion statement. During the reign of Henry III of France in the late sixteenth century, the King inspired a trend among his countrymen when he took to wearing a curly wig to cover his balding pate. The trend jumped the Channel and Elizabeth I was said to have owned more than eighty wigs, worn to conceal her thinning grey hair. The popular "full bottomed" styles of the seventeeth century were ruthlessly satirized by Hogarth.

While the firm can be traced to 1689, it was named Ede and Ravenscroft around the time Joseph Webb Ede married Rosanna Ravenscroft, in 1871. The main shop in Chancery Lane—the epicenter of legal London—was built around 1890 and retains much of its fine cabinetry and fixtures even after a 1992 restoration. It's a hushed place, and while the shop now sells everyday suits and shirts and accessories, a sense of import and solemnity remains.

Emma Hope

EST. 1986

53 SLOANE SQUARE, SW1

☎ 020 7259 9566 ⊖ SLOANE SQUARE

www.emmahope.co.uk

TUESDAY TO FRIDAY 10AM TO 6PM; SATURDAY 10AM TO 6PM;
CLOSED SUNDAY

"REGALIA FOR FEET" IS SHOE DESIGNER EMMA HOPE'S MOTTO, AND IT IS EMBROIDERED ON THE INSOLE OF every shoe she makes. A fashion-writer mother and an obsession with rummage sales and old shoes led Hope to study at Cordwainers, London's renowned shoemaking school, in the 1980s. Soon after she opened her first shop in Islington, and right away began to win awards for her whimsical, vintage inspired shoes. Hope defends quality and design against mass manufacturing: Her shoes are made in small family-owned factories in Tuscany, and the rich embroidery and beading often found on her shoes and ballet flats are handmade by specialist craftspeople.

Today, Londoners have two other locations in which to pick up Hope's styles, including her Sloane Square shop, a bright, comfortable space with cream velvet benches and white walls behind a terracotta and black-painted facade. There she sells everything from sumptuous boots (with reasonable heels!) and bags to sneakers based on old-school plimsoles (available in leather, crushed velvet, and printed pony skin).

Freed of London

EST. 1928

94 ST. MARTIN'S LANE, WC2

☎ 020 7240 0432 ⊖ LEICESTER SQUARE

www.freedoflondon.com

MONDAY TO FRIDAY 9:30AM TO 5:30PM;

SATURDAY 9:30AM TO 3:30PM; CLOSED SUNDAY

A CENTURY AGO, LONDON-BASED GAMBA WAS ONE OF THE MOST POPULAR POINTE SHOE MAKERS IN THE DANCE world. In 1928, two of its employees, Frederick and Dora Freed, left to establish their own shoe company in St. Martin's Lane, the heart of London's theater district. For almost twenty years they hand-crafted and sold

shoes from the basement of a shop, before growing popularity demanded they open a storefront just down the street, at number 94. Gamba's loss was the ballet world's gain. Today, Freed supplies the pointe shoes for the English National and the Royal Ballet companies, and to ballerinas all over the world— about forty percent of all ballet shoes are custom made by Freed.

Given the amount of labor and customization pointe shoes require, it may be surpris-

ing to learn that before each performance Anna Pavlova tore hers apart and almost ritualistically reassembled them before taking the stage, and that Darcy Bussell takes a special hammer to her shoes to break them in. At Freed's East London factory, the "turn-shoe technique" is used: Shoes are formed inside-out and then turned for shaping and finishing. More traditional styles (and those custom made) are assembled over a period of days using three pieces of satin for the uppers, a sole cut from a leather sheet by hand, and a toeblock made of paper, burlap, and paste before it is "baked" to harden overnight. Each of Freed's thirty shoemakers has an individual maker's mark to stamp into the shoe—a tradition started by Freed so he could trace a complaint about a particular shoe—and which today makes preferential reordering by ballerinas easier.

Harvie & Hudson

EST. 1947

77 AND 97 JERMYN STREET, SW1

☎ 020 7839 3578 ⊖ GREEN PARK

www.harvieandhudson.com

MONDAY TO SATURDAY 9:30AM TO 6PM; CLOSED SUNDAY

JERMYN STREET MUST BE THE MOST FAMOUS PLACE IN THE WORLD FOR MEN TO BUY SHIRTS. BUT OF ALL THE SHOPS to sell fine ready- or custom-made shirts, Harvie & Hudson is the only Jermyn Street shirtmaker that still makes its shirts on site. Given sky-rocketing rents, it's a testament to the firm's heritage and its dedicated customers that it can keep the manufacturing so close to home.

The business is still in the families of the original founders Thomas Harvie and George Hudson, who learned the trade by making uniforms during World War I. Upstairs at number 97, in a room overlooking the churchyard of St. James's, there are six sewing stations where all bespoke shirts are made using twenty-four pieces of fabric. They cost about £150 each. An initial order of four shirts must be placed and takes about ten weeks to fulfill. Separate collars, even separate cuffs, are offered along with a huge range of stripes and pastels. Off-the-peg shirts start at about £70 and come with Harvie & Hudson's trademark mother-of-pearl buttons, Kent cut-away collars, and generous length.

James Lock and Co.

EST. 1676 👑👑

6 ST. JAMES'S STREET, SW1

☎ 020 7930 8874   ⊖ GREEN PARK

www.lockhatters.co.uk

MONDAY TO FRIDAY 9AM TO 5:30PM; SATURDAY 9:30AM TO 5PM;
CLOSED SUNDAY

TEN YEARS AFTER THE GREAT FIRE OF 1666, HAT MAKER ROBERT DAVIS ESTABLISHED A SHOP IN ST. JAMES'S Street. The business was later undertaken by his son and later still by his grandson-in-law, George James Locke, in 1759, by which time St. James's had become the most fashionable shopping district in London. Perfectly placed, the shop soon became an extension of St. James's eighteenth-century coffee house and club culture.

In the seventeenth century hat-making as a trade was broken down into separate components: there were cap-makers, felters, hat-banders, and milliners. Simple caps, for example, would be made entirely on a cap-maker's premises and later "finished" by a hatter to the customer's specific needs of styling, trimming, and moulding. Finishing was unique to the best hatters and their talent was sought out by aristocrats (who often lavished more on their servants' headgear than their own) and politicians for the qualities that distinguished a hatter from a mere hat seller.

Lock's became the place to go for the chapeau bras, or "arm hat," a hat that was ostentatiously carried under the arm, rather than worn. Depictions of it can be seen as late as the 1930s. (The Lock family themselves weren't fond of the affectation, calling it "dishonest.") Lock also designed caps for the miltary—they sent Nelson to Trafalgar and Wellington to Waterloo in Lock hats. They have fitted countless top hats (or "silk hats" as they were known) and offer restoration and refitting of them; and they famously supplied a velvet hat for Oscar Wilde to wear on his American tour. Hatfitting is still done with the help of a *conformateur*, a French-made device of wooden pegs that adjusts to the contour of the head and records it by pinpricks on a small white card.

There is no question that the grey top hat, known as the Ascot and sported only once a year at that famous horse race, was invented at Lock's. Owners would even store theirs at the shop between seasons. But there is controversy as to whether it was Lock who invented that swiftly fading symbol of London, the bowler hat. It is said that Lock made a hat at the time called a Coke (pronounced "cook"), named after the customer who ordered it, William Coke. In 1850, Coke was looking for something comfortable and casual for hunting to be modeled on a rounded game-keepers cap but more resilient. Naturally, Lock obliged. However, since Lock was a hatter and not a hat-maker, the task of manufacturing the cap was given to Lock's chief felt supplier, Thomas and William Bowler, who were hat-makers in their own right as well. Bowler was based in Southwark, and from then on the hat was known as a "bowler" south of the Thames and a "coke" north of the river.

While the business has changed hands numerous times in its long existence, it has always been looked after by a descendant of the Lock family. In 1765, Lock's moved just across the street from its original family-leased premises to number 6 St. James's, where it still operates today. Once an alehouse known as The Feathers, the shop front is typical Regency, and today a Grade-II listed building. Inside, the rectangular coffin staircase (so named because it was designed to allow a coffin to be carried out of the residence) in the back still connects the shop to what was once living quarters upstairs and incorporates workshops today. Ready-made hats—for men and women—are reasonably priced given their extraordinary quality. Custom orders are accommodated too. Coke hats—bowlers—run about £225.

Jasper Conran

36 SACKVILLE STREET, W1

☎ 020 7292 9080   ⊖ PICCADILLY CIRCUS

www.jasperconran.com

MONDAY TO FRIDAY 10:30AM TO 6:30PM;

SATURDAY 11AM TO 6PM; CLOSED SUNDAY

JASPER CONRAN CASTS SUCH A BROAD SHADOW OVER CON-
TEMPORARY BRITISH DESIGN THAT IT IS ALMOST EASIER
to list the things he *doesn't* design. The multitalented son of Terence
Conran (see page 65) began designing in the 1970s and applied it to nearly
everything he could get his hands on: elegant evening clothes, wallpaper
and Wedgwood china, costume and set designs for London theaters.

The best of Jasper Conran's fine clothing, luxurious bedding, and
designs for Waterford crystal and Wedgwood china are available at his
Mayfair store. The restored Georgian house, which dates from the 1730s,
features lovely period details, including the main staircase and fireplaces;
walls are painted in subtle taupe and sand. The classic cuts of Conran's
English tailored suits are displayed in the gentlemanly parlor, bespoke
furniture is arranged in the salon, and linens are laid out on fine furniture in the upstairs bedrooms. The lovely view of the formal garden,
which Conran designed himself, is not to be missed.

65

John Lobb

EST. 1849 ♛♛♛

9 ST. JAMES'S STREET, SW1

☎ 020 7930 3664 ⊖ GREEN PARK

www.johnlobb.co.uk

MONDAY TO FRIDAY 9AM TO 5:30PM; SATURDAY 9AM TO 4:30PM;
CLOSED SUNDAY

"THE LAST SHALL BE FIRST": JOHN LOBB'S MOTTO, ALONG WITH ANTIQUE SHOES, SHOEHORNS, AND BUCKLES IN museum-like cases, are all in evidence here. It seems a modest shop, but Lobb shods Queen Elizabeth II, Prince Philip, and Prince Charles, and custom-made shoes even for the more pedestrian among us start at £2,000. Six craftsmen work on a single pair of shoes: the fitter, the last-maker (who carves the foot-shaped lasts from a single block of wood), the clicker (who chooses the eight pieces of leather that go into each shoe), the closer (who does the cutting and sewing), the maker (who adds the sole), and the polisher (who finishes the shoe). If you choose to go the custom route—from Scottish brogues to velvet slippers and

Wellington boots—expect a wait of up to twelve weeks. Those lighter of wallet may choose to visit the ready-to-wear shop a few blocks away on Jermyn Street.

Lobb was from Cornwall and learned the trade from his father. His exceptional gift for making fine shoes earned him awards at various Victorian international exhibitions. He eventually became the proud holder of a Royal Warrant as Bootmaker to Edward, Prince of Wales, and retained it when he became King Edward VII. Lobb has held at least one Royal Warrant ever since and currently holds three.

The bay window and wooden shopfront conceal a surprisingly small, hushed space decorated simply with old stuffed chairs and an Oriental rug, the air redolent of wood shavings and leather. Individual lasts are numbered, tagged, and boxed in an archive downstairs and up on the balcony.

Margaret Howell

EST. 1970

34 WIGMORE STREET, W1

☎ 020 7009 9009 ⊖ BOND STREET

www.margarethowell.co.uk

MONDAY, TUESDAY, WEDNESDAY, FRIDAY 10AM TO 6PM; THURS-
DAY 10AM TO 7PM; SATURDAY 10AM TO 6PM; CLOSED SUNDAY

THE CLEAN LINES, DIFFUSED NATURAL LIGHT, AND COLORS THAT DOMINATE THE MARGARET HOWELL FLAGSHIP SHOP manifest the clothing designer's taste for simplicity and fine detail. Howell has said, "My pieces are more like applied arts. It's like designing a chair: I want something that will stick around." The bright, minimalist shop showcases both men's and women's clothes.

Howell started out designing men's shirts in 1970 from a studio in Blackheath, southeast London; her first women's collection was unveiled ten years later. The Wigmore Street shop opened in 2002. Her clothes often use interpretations of old British prints and styling, and the winter line is always dominated by fine tweed from the Highlands.

In keeping with her commitment to classic British design of all disciplines, Margaret Howell has also collaborated with the British furniture firm Ercol to reissue some classic 1950s pieces—the Butterfly and Stacking chairs, Plank dining table, and Trio nesting tables—which are also available at Heal's (see page 109).

Paul Smith

EST. 1970 🦁

122 KENSINGTON PARK ROAD W11

☎ 020 727 3558   ⊖ NOTTING HILL GATE

www.paulsmith.co.uk

MONDAY TO THURSDAY 10:30AM TO 6:30PM; FRIDAY AND
SATURDAY 10AM TO 6:30PM; CLOSED SUNDAY

NOTTINGHAM NATIVE PAUL SMITH YEARNED TO BE A PRO-
FESSIONAL CYCLIST BUT FOUND HIS TRUE CALLING AFTER
an accident put a halt to his dreams. Even though his father made him
find work in a clothing factory as a teen, it was the time he spent at a
Nottingham pub, where students from the local fashion college hung out,
that convinced him to pursue a new career path. His collections are still
designed in Nottingham and London, and much is still manufactured in
England. Smith's elegantly tailored clothes usually come with a twist: A
slim men's suit comes lined in his trademark wave of stripes; a woman's
navy overcoat reveals a dash of pink at the wrists and collar; and whimsical floral shirts abound in the men's casual collection. Smith is always
witty, yet never strays far from classic.

Although there are Paul Smith shops all over the world, he deserves
special mention here not only for his commitment to English styling but
also for the ways his London shops play with traditional English architecture. The Mayfair shop is notable less for the juxtaposition of its modern

architecture on an old street than for its unusual collection of furniture, and the new shop behind Borough Market (see page 283) is in a deep oddly shaped warehouse room where produce was probably once stored. But the shop in Kensington Park Road, which reinterprets six rooms of a traditional Notting Hill residence, is perhaps the finest. The women's collection is in the Kensington Room on the ground floor; men's accessories are tucked under the glass-top of a dining table in the dining room; children's clothes and are toys jumbled in the playroom upstairs; and bespoke services are available on the top floor in the Guston Room, with bottles of buttons and bolts of fabric and patterns scattered artfully around like an old tailor's shop.

Stephen Jones

EST. 1980

36 GREAT QUEEN STREET, WC2

☎ 020 7242 0770 ⊖ HOLBORN

www.stephenjonesmillinery.com

TUESDAY TO FRIDAY 11AM TO 6PM;

CLOSED SATURDAY AND SUNDAY

AS A STUDENT AT THE LEGENDARY CENTRAL ST. MARTIN'S ART SCHOOL IN THE 1970S, STEPHEN JONES WAS ALREADY known as a "millinery magician." His taste for unusual materials (copper mesh, fresh flowers, fur) has won him commissions from leading fashion houses and designers John Galliano, Comme des Garçons, and Jasper Conran (see page 65). He was included in the FIT's "Fashion and Surrealism" exhibit and his work is in the permanent collections of the Louvre, the Victoria & Albert Museum, and the Kyoto Costume Institute.

Despite being one of leading couture milliners for royalty and celebrities, Jones offers whimsical but wearable hats in ranges called Miss Jones and Jonesboy at his Covent Garden shop. While not exactly custom made, they must be ordered, take up to three weeks to complete, and cost around £100.

Situated between a florist and a shop selling Masonic paraphernalia, the shop's minimal window display belies the hive of activity in the workshop at the back of the store, where the hats are still handmade.

Tracey Neuls

EST. 2005

29 MARYLEBONE LANE, W1

☎ 020 7935 0039 ⊖ BOND STREET · *www.tn29.com*

MONDAY, TUESDAY, WEDNESDAY, AND FRIDAY 11AM TO 6:30PM;
THURSDAY 11AM TO 8PM; SATURDAY NOON TO 5PM;
CLOSED SUNDAY

ON A LOVELY CORNER OF MARYLEBONE LANE (SEE PAUL ROTHE; PAGE TK) TRACEY NEULS OCCUPIES ONE OF THE most perfect shopfronts in London. Her beautifully designed women's shoes—unusual, but far from unwearable—take pride of place here. Trained at Cordwainers, London's famous footwear and leatherworking college, Neuls has transcended the use of fixtures, cases, and shelves.

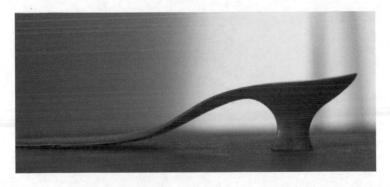

Instead, one of each of her designs for the season hangs softly by ribbons at eye level from the ceiling, creating the effect of walking into an environment rather than a shop. The shoes are of exquisite design and quality—soft leathers, colors rarely used on shoes (an unusual matte gold, teal, and a pretty, peachy pink) and include charming embellishments like ribbons and fastenings. Each box purchased is wrapped in orange paper by the shop assistant, and in place of bags, adhesive handles are placed on each package for easy carrying. Almost as much care is taken in presentation as in the crafting of each pair of shoes.

Turnbull & Asser

EST. 1885 ♔

71-72 JERMYN STREET, SW1

☎ 020 7808 3000   ⊖ GREEN PARK

www.turnbullandasser.com

MONDAY TO FRIDAY 9AM TO 6PM; SATURDAY 9:30AM TO 6PM;

CLOSED SUNDAY

NAMED AFTER THE SEVENTEENTH-CENTURY EARL OF ST. ALBANS, HENRY JERMYN, JERMYN STREET IS STILL THE commercial heart of St. James's, where privileged, club-going gentlemen are suited, shod, and shaved. There may be no better description of the area than Nikolaus Pevsner's when he described it as having "the special masculine atmosphere that comes with tradition and gradual change."

Some of the shops have modernized in an attempt to shake off Jermyn Street's musty ambience, but the names haven't changed at all: Harvie & Hudson (see page 61), Russell & Bromley, George F. Trumper (see page 43), and Turnbull and Asser, whose Edwardian shopfront on Jermyn Street looks like something out of an English country village: Walnut window surrounds and leaded glass, colorfully planted window

White Evening Bows

Pre-Tied Bows

Black Single En...

boxes, and orginal brass lettering advertising themselves as "Hosiers & Glovers" and "Shirtmakers."

It is the shirts that Turnbull & Asser is best known for. It has a Royal Warrant for providing Prince Charles with his shirts (and, rumor has it, even a bespoke sling for his arm when he suffered a polo injury some years ago). Even the filmed James Bond always wears Turnbull & Asser shirts: his preferred style, known colloquially as the "Bond shirt," is made of Sea Island cotton, has the firm's standard spread collar (slightly deeper than a typical spread collar), and—since Sean Connery appeared in *Dr. No* in 1962— a two-button turnback cuff with mother-of-pearl buttons (this model runs about £180). The firm also provided the film studio MGM with the hundreds of shirts that spilled out of Gatsby's closet in the 1974 film version of *The Great Gatsby*.

While still a bastion of the aristrocratic British male, Turnbull & Asser also make ladies shirts, and the smart stripes they're known for are also turned into robes and pyjamas. (For soldiers on the front during the First World War, the firm even invented the Oilsilk Combination Cover-all & Ground Sheet, a raincoat that doubled as a sleeping bag.)

Vivienne Westwood
World's End

EST. 1970

430 KING'S ROAD, SW10

☎ 020 7352 6551   ⊖ SLOANE SQUARE

www.viviennewestwood.co.uk

MONDAY, TUESDAY, WEDNESDAY, FRIDAY 10AM TO 5PM;

THURSDAY 11AM TO 6PM; SATURDAY 11AM TO 6PM;

CLOSED SUNDAY

THE GRITTIER END OF CHELSEA'S KING'S ROAD, IN THE SHADOW OF THE TOWERS OF THE WORLD'S END HOUSING estate, was home to the unlikely pairing of London's hippie and punk movements in the late 1960s and 1970s. Across the street from where a hippie faction known as Gandalf's Garden published a magazine featuring the poetry of Christopher Logue beside articles like "The Glastonbury Mystique: Jesus and the Druids," Vivienne Westwood and Malcolm McLaren ran punk's fashion emporium under a giant pink rubber sign that read SEX. What had started as a modest record shop in the back of a garage where Westwood made drainpipe trousers and velvet jackets for "teddy boys" became the punk movement's HQ.

After years of dressing the New York Dolls and Sex Pistols in her S&M-inspired clothes, Westwood held her first formal runway show in 1981, when she also renamed the shop "World's End." Around this time Westwood's fascination with historical English dress and tailoring techniques emerged; all of her subsequent collections have featured fine Harris tweeds, tartans, crown insignias, and corsets in playful reinterpretations of classic British fabrics and styles. Long tartan skirts are set apart by dramatic diagonal hems, and cardigans are cut a touch too tight. Her trademark red hair and crimson lipstick have made Westwood an icon herself, and she was recently given a retrospective by the Victoria & Albert Museum.

Savile Row

SAVILE ROW IN MAYFAIR WAS LAID OUT BEGINNING IN THE 1730s AS PART OF THE LORD BURLINGTON'S ESTATE; IT is named after Dorothy Savile, the wife of the 3rd Earl of Burlington. Fashionable tailors began moving into the area in the late eighteenth century; Beau Brummel, that most famous of dandies, took his business there, and before long so did gentlemen from all over Europe. James Poole, a tailor in Regent Street, moved to old Burlington Street in 1823 and quickly expanded his workshop into the neighboring street—Savile Row. His son Henry Poole took up the reins of the business, and dominated the bespoke trade for the rest of the nineteenth century. By the 1830s, Savile Row was famous for its tailoring and particularly its "bespoke" service.

The term bespoke dates to the seventeenth century, when tailors kept whole lengths of a particular cloth on their premises; when a customer chose a particular cloth, the entire bolt was said to have "been spoken for." Bespoke differs from "made-to-measure," which uses a template pattern of a suit that is then adjusted, with less exactness, to a customer's measurements. Bespoke, by contrast, requires more than twenty individual measurements and other shaping details to be taken before a suit is tailored. One of the older firms on the street, Kilgour, claims that it takes more than eighty hours of tailoring to make one of its suits.

More than 7,000 suits are made on Savile Row every year by specialized shops that together employ more than a hundred tailors, fitters, and cutters. But many Savile Row suits today are cut elsewhere; the prices of precious real estate necessitates it, and the shops know that the days of busy downstairs workshops are numbered. While the tailors compete for business, they also share secondary services, such as cloth and notion suppliers. Their proximity facilitates the training of new tailors and cutters, as the process of learning bespoke suit-fitting takes so long—up to five years—that apprentices must move around to different houses for training opportunities.

Recently, a large group of Savile Row tailors organized a demonstration against the encroachment of High Street shops in their discreet Mayfair district that took advantage of Savile Row's name and reputation. Threatened by ever-rising rents in an area some developers think ripe for growth and landlords consider ripe for bigger profits, 150 tailors, bedecked in their finest English Cuts, scissors in hand and measuring tapes around their necks, took to the streets to draw attention to the threat posed against Savile Row's iconic British status.

While developers took their own measure of the area, Westminster Council officials backed Savile Row, announcing that tailoring could be classified as "light industry" and therefore forestalling any change-of-use applications from chain retailers. In another move to fend off commercial development, it is also possible that the tailoring workshops may be registered as English Heritage-listed properties.

However, Savile Row faces other threats. Long-established firm Anderson and Shepherd has been abandoned by Prince Charles, who now gets his shirts made to measure at Turnbull & Asser (see page 76). They have lost a Royal Warrant, and recently moved to Old Burlington Street to find cheaper rent. But it's not all bad news. Henry Poole, a fixture on

Savile Row since 1846, recently negotiated an agreement to remain there for another fifteen years.

Note that what is known as Savile Row includes not only the street itself but also nearby Clifford Street, Conduit Street, Cork Street, Old Burlington Street, and Sackville Street. In all, Savile Row constitutes about fifty firms; five of the finest are:

ANDERSON AND SHEPPARD

EST. 1873

32 Old Burlington Street, W1

☎ 020 7734 1420

www.anderson-sheppard.co.uk

DEGE & SKINNER

EST. 1865 ♛

10 Savile Row, W1

☎ 020 7734 8794

www.degesavilerow.co.uk

HENRY POOLE

EST. 1846

15 Savile Row, W1

☎ 020 7734 5985

www.henrypoole.co.uk

H. HUNTSMAN & SONS
EST. 1849
11 Savile Row, W1
☎ 020 7734 7441
www.h-huntsman.com

KILGOUR
EST. 1882
8 Savile Row, W1
☎ 020 7734 6905
www.8savilerow.com

COFFEE ROASTERS &
TEA MERCHANTS

Angelucci

EST. 1929

23B FRITH STREET, W1

☎ 020 7437 5889   ⊖ LEICESTER SQUARE

MONDAY, TUESDAY, WEDNESDAY 9AM TO 5PM; THURSDAY 9AM
TO 1PM; FRIDAY AND SATURDAY 9AM TO 5PM; CLOSED SUNDAY

THE MINISCULE, NO-FRILLS ANGELUCCI STORE HAS ROASTED SOME OF THE BEST COFFEE BEANS IN LONDON FOR MORE than seventy-five years. The Angeluccis arrived in London in the 1910s and opened the shop that their children Alma and Andy still run today. During the Second World War their father was interned as an enemy alien—as were many London Italians—but their mother kept the store running and kept customers like French-born, Allied spy Odette Churchill and the exiled Charles de Gaulle in coffee beans.

Today, Angelucci's main business is supplying many Soho restaurants with coffee beans and sending their Mokital blend to Bar Italia a few doors down. But the tiny shop welcomes walk-in customers. Under the original pendant lights are sacks of twenty or thirty different beans; on the warping counter the beans are weighed on a red enamel scale and, if you wish, ground in the matching grinder. Alas, the threat of chain coffee shops and rising Soho rents puts Angelucci (and their neighbor, the Algerian Coffee Stores on Old Compton Street) at a worrisome risk. But the owners are never anything but cheerful.

H.R. Higgins

EST. 1942 ♛

DUKE STREET, W1

☎ 020 7629 3913 ⊖ BOND STREET

www.hrhiggins.co.uk

MONDAY TO FRIDAY 9:30AM TO 5:30PM;

SATURDAY 10AM TO 5PM; CLOSED SUNDAY

H.R. HIGGINS ESTABLISHED A WHOLESALE COFFEE BUSI-NESS IN 1942. ROASTING BEANS IN AN ATTIC ON SOUTH Moulton Street, he supplied coffee to merchants whose storefront businesses had been disrupted by the business of war. In 1944 he opened a retail storefront of his own. He did the roasting in the basement.

Today the firm conducts its wholesale business from Waltham Abbey, just north of London, and roasts all of its beans there. But the retail business continues, having moved to Mayfair, where a third generation of Higginses now offers specialty teas alongside almost fifty varieties of coffee. Coffee beans and loose teas—stored in shiny copper tins—are weighed on an old-fashioned balance, packaged in Higgins' signature brown bags, and tied with string. Their elegant blue-and-red gift boxes can be filled with a mix of tea and coffee and sent anywhere.

Downstairs is a (sadly, uninspiring) small tasting room and café, where nevertheless excellent coffee and tea can be had for half the price of the chain cafés of nearby Oxford Street.

R. Twining & Co.

EST. 1706 ☙☙

216 STRAND, WC2

☎ 020 7353 3511　⊖ CHANCERY LANE

www.twinings.com

MONDAY TO FRIDAY 9:30AM TO 4:30PM; SATURDAY 10AM TO
4:30PM; CLOSED SUNDAY

THE ENGLISH LOVE OF TEA IS A SURPRISINGLY RECENT DEVELOPMENT. COFFEE, WHICH IS SAID TO HAVE BEEN introduced in the mid-seventeenth century by a Greek student at Oxford, was for a long time far more popular. Coffee houses sprang up all over London; the oldest of them became the focal points for political life, eventually transforming themselves into gentleman's clubs.

Even Twining's, famed around the world today for its tea, was itself originally a coffee house. Founded by Thomas Twining in 1706, it served coffee—and brandy and spa water—in the small Devereaux Court to the side of today's Strand shop.

Twining was thirty-one when he became master of Tom's Coffee House, at the "sign of the golden lion." Having apprenticed to a wealthy East India merchant in the 1690s, Twining was perfectly placed to take advantage of the East India Company's growth and influence in promoting new products from the colonies, including tea. The near unregulated expansion of the tea trade (what the Company imported accounted for more than half of all tea sold at the time) led Twining to shift the focus of his business from coffee to tea in the mid-eighteenth century despite the heavy duties applied that made it a drink only for the rich.

The narrow shop in the Strand is said to be smallest shopfront in London. It was designed by Richard Twining, the founder's grandson, in 1787. Richard had earlier been responsible for the Tea Duty Commutation Act of 1784, which dramatically lowered the duty. Tea sales soared among all social classes in the nineteenth century and became the drink most associated with England. In fact, tea trading was so robust that Twining's opened a branch in the City, in 1874, just to be closer to the markets.

Today it is known as London's oldest shop to be run continuously from the same location and by the same family. It received its first Royal Warrant in 1911. Until the 1930s it was common for customers to have their teas custom blended to their tastes (recipes were kept on record in the shop). Customers today have to make do with a selection of pre-packed loose and bagged teas.

DEPARTMENT STORES &
HOME FURNISHERS

Celia Birtwell

EST. 1984

71 WESTBOURNE PARK ROAD, W2

☎ 020 7721 0877 ⊖ WESTBOURNE PARK

www.celiabirtwell.com

MONDAY, TUESDAY, WEDNESDAY, FRIDAY 10AM TO 5PM;
THURSDAY 11AM TO 6PM; SATURDAY BY APPOINTMENT;
CLOSED SUNDAY

I N 1970, CELIA BIRTWELL WAS IMMORTALIZED BY THE ARTIST DAVID HOCKNEY IN *MR. AND MRS. CLARK AND PERCY*, a double portrait of Birtwell and her then-husband, the fashion designer Ossie Clark. They were at the height of their careers: Along with Biba and Mary Quant, Clark's dresses and suits helped define the look of Swinging London, and Birtwell hand printed many of his fabrics—patterns with names like "Golden Slumbers" and "Mystic Daisy."

It wasn't long after Hockney painted them that Clark and Birtwell's personal and professional lives began to diverge. Their business partnership and their marriage ended, and Ossie Clark eventually went bankrupt. In the 1980s, Birtwell returned to designing textiles and opened her own boutique and atelier in Westborne Park Road, on the northern edge of Notting Hill. The understated façade of her shop—today run by her son and daughter-in-law—seems at odds with her fanciful animal prints and botanical designs, but once inside it reveals itself to be an archive of

Birtwell's clever talent. Her fabric designs cover the walls, cleanly set off by the lacquered moldings; tables and chests are stacked with bolts of her colorful textiles; a Queen Anne chair is whimsically covered in Birtwell's very first furnishing pattern, the remarkably successful "Animal Solo," a sixteenth-century-inspired pattern in rich maroon or charcoal on linen or cotton. Those trademark animals now appear in other designs, too, such as "Animal Trellis" and "Kew."

Bespoke orders can be taken from a selection of archived designs. For those not ready to reupholster their living rooms, the shop also sells silk scarves printed with some of Birtwell's patterns for about £95.

The Conran Shop

EST. 1973

81 FULHAM ROAD, SW3

☎ 020 7589 7401   ⊖ SOUTH KENSINGTON

www.conranshop.co.uk

MONDAY, TUESDAY, FRIDAY 10AM TO 6PM; WEDNESDAY AND
THURSDAY 10AM TO 7PM; SATURDAY 10AM TO 6:30PM;
SUNDAY NOON TO 4PM

ORIGINALLY TRAINED AS AN ARCHITECT, TERENCE CONRAN HAS BEEN A LEADING DESIGNER—AND CHAMpion of a humane, holistic vision of good domestic design—for more than 50 years. After working in an architecture office and designing textiles in the 1950s, Conran opened a café on the King's Road, sold furniture he designed from a basement shop in the Piccadilly Arcade, designed exhibitions, and was an early promoter of corporate identity design.

Conran's earliest foray into retail was a home furnishings store in a former pub on Fulham Road, founded in 1964 and called Habitat. Staff had their

hair cut by Vidal Sassoon, wore uniforms designed by Mary Quant, and flat-pack (or assemble-at-home furniture) made its debut. The concept was an immediate success, and within three years there were four more Habitat shops across London (a number still remain, but are now owned by IKEA). In 1973, the original Habitat was renamed The Conran Shop.

In 1985, Conran set out on an ambitious restoration of the Michelin Tire headquarters just across the street from his first store. It is a hugely imaginative building of no particular style. Built in 1911, it's an amalgam of stained glass, mosaic, glazed brick, Art Nouveau, and functionalism. On the façade and floors tile mosaics portray famous racing victories achieved on Michelin tires. A stained glass Bibendum, the Michelin Man himself, can be seen "drinking" a cup of sharp objects—an allusion to Michelin's motto that their tires "drink up obstacles." Behind the vivid exterior is a minimal glass box housing the shop designed by Conran's architectural and design practice.

Today The Conran Shop sells a selection of contemporary furniture, design objects, home furnishings, jewelry, bath products, picture frames, and lighting fixtures. One of Conran's many restaurants, Bibendum, is upstairs; an oyster and seafood bar perches in the vaulted Fulham Road entrance to the building.

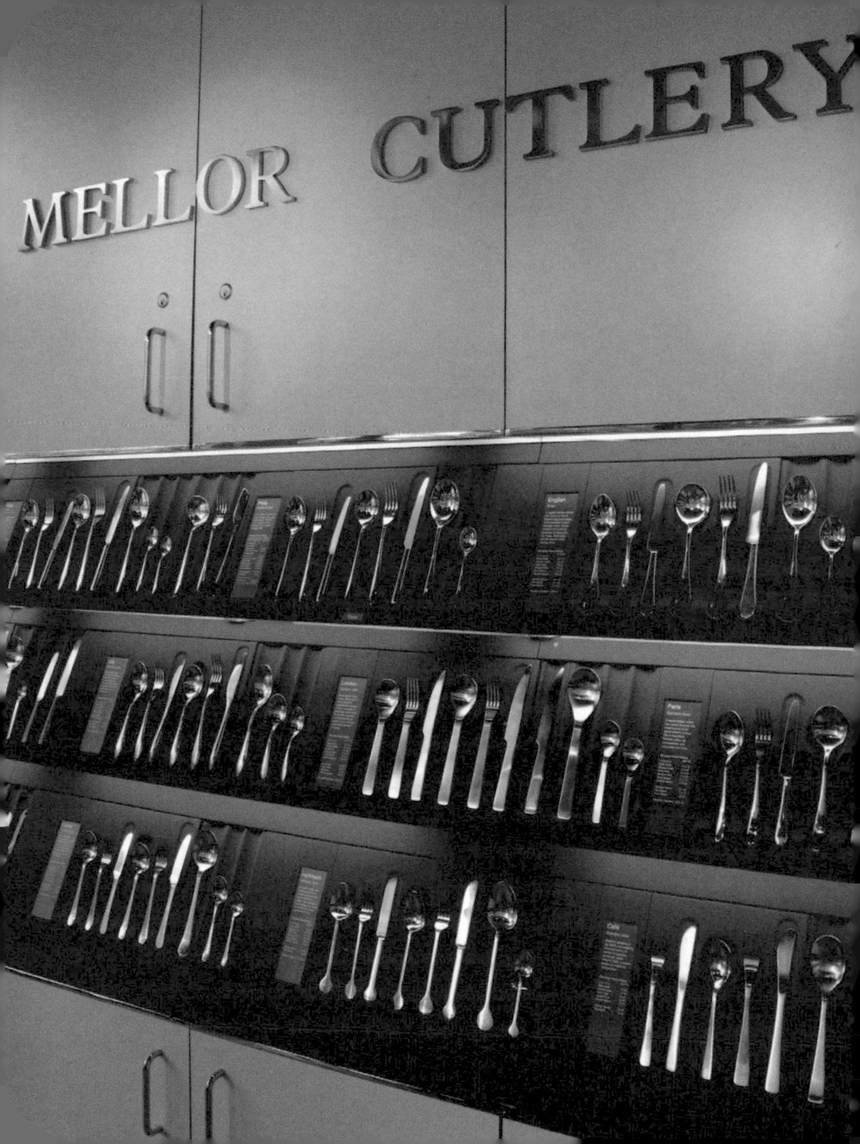
MELLOR CUTLERY

David Mellor

EST. 1969

4 SLOANE SQUARE, SW1

☎ 020 7730 4259 ⊖ SLOANE SQUARE

www.davidmellordesign.com

MONDAY TO SATURDAY 9:30AM TO 6PM; SUNDAY 11AM TO 5PM

THE RENOWNED CUTLERY DESIGNER DAVID MELLOR WAS BORN IN SHEFFIELD, HOME TO BRITAIN'S ONCE GREAT steel industry and its close cousin, the Sheffield plate cutlery industry. While a student at an art school there, he was recruited by the Royal College of Art in London, where he developed a taste for modern design and honed his skills for the detailed perfectionism that epitomizes his work today. All of Mellor's silverware—from his original "Pride" place settings (designed when he was still a student) to his Georgian-style "English" and sculptural "City" designs—are made in a small purpose-built factory in Derbyshire.

Mellor opened his Sloane Square shop in 1969. He originally envisioned it as a modern hardware store where he could sell his highly designed flatware and Wedgwood china alongside ordinary nails and paint. But the shop today, a bright, modern store in the heart of London, focuses on his sleek designs and a selection of high-end kitchenware. It exemplifies British design at its best.

Fortnum & Mason

EST. 1707

181 PICCADILLY, W1

☎ 020 7734 8040 ⏣ PICCADILLY CIRCUS

www.fortnumandmason.com

MONDAY TO SATURDAY 10AM TO 6:30PM

SUNDAY NOON TO 6PM (FOOD HALL ONLY)

IN 1707, THE ACT OF UNION WITH SCOTLAND MARKED THE ESTABLISHMENT OF GREAT BRITAIN. THAT SAME YEAR A footman in the royal household named William Fortnum and a stall-holder in St. James's Market named Hugh Mason joined forces to open a general goods and grocery store. But it wasn't until 1773 that the present store was officially established on this Piccadilly corner by one of their descendents, who registered it as a grocery store and tea dealer. With strong family ties to the East India Company, it is no wonder that Fortnum & Mason became known for its tea. It was in great part responsible for introducing the food and spices of Britain's growing empire to London during the eighteenth century. In 1886, the shop was the first to sell Heinz baked beans (today a staple British food if ever there was one), and it supplied food for the George Mallory-led expedition to Mount Everest in 1922, including sixty cans of quail in foie gras and forty-eight bottles of champagne. (The team didn't make the summit, but did achieve the highest climb to date.)

The grand Piccadilly premises were built between 1926 and 1928 in a Neo-Georgian style and painted the now-trademark Fortnum & Mason blue. A red-carpeted oak staircase leads upstairs to the homewares and toy departments, but it is the food hall that Fortnum & Mason is best known for. Ingredients sourced from the best producers around the world are prepared into house-label preserves (rose petal jam), condiments (prickly bee honey), and sweets. Towering displays of food wrapped in the firm's distinctive packaging are set beneath crystal chandeliers on long mahogany shelving units.

Fortnum & Mason also houses three restaurants: The Fountain is famous for its ice cream sundaes, including the Knickerbocker Glory (ice cream, jam, fruit, nuts, and whipped cream). The Patio in the mezzanine over the food hall serves oysters and an all-day brunch menu. On the top level of the store is The St. James's, good for afternoon tea.

General Trading Company

EST. 1920 👑👑👑

2 SYMONS STREET, SW3

☎ 020 7730 0411 ⊖ SLOANE SQUARE

www.general-trading.co.uk

MONDAY, TUESDAY, THURSDAY, FRIDAY 10AM TO 6:30PM;

WEDNESDAY 10AM TO 7PM; SATURDAY 10AM TO 6:30PM;

CLOSED SUNDAY

THE DECOMMISSIONED FIREHOUSE THAT THE GENERAL TRADING COMPANY STORE HAS OCCUPIED SINCE 2004 MAY be the only space in Chelsea large enough to contain its enormous selection of goods. Its lofty prices may reflect its Royal Warrants, as well as its reputation as the first stop for newlywed "Sloane Rangers." But General Trading offers more than wedding registries.

Eclecticism is the rule here. The shop features multiple rooms with much of the stock arranged like the unloaded cargo of a Dutch East India Trading ship. There are Eastern-inspired lacquered chairs across the room from a French antique brass bed while a Chinese cupboard filled with Victorian glass perfume bottles shares space with a pair of mid-century modern armchairs. There is a room full of elegantly packaged toiletries, a whole section devoted to gift wrapping and cards, and an enormous selection of crystal and china.

Harrods

EST. 1853

87–135 BROMPTON ROAD, SW1

☎ 020 7730 1234   ⊖ KNIGHTSBRIDGE

www.harrods.com

MONDAY TO SATURDAY 10AM TO 8PM; SUNDAY NOON TO 6PM

HARRODS BILLS ITSELF AS "THE MOST FAMOUS DEPART-MENT STORE IN THE WORLD," BUT MOST LONDONERS have only a passing acquaintance with the store. It may be better known for being owned by the father of Dodi al-Fayed, the late Princess Diana's boyfriend, than as the place where writer A. A. Milne found the bear that inspired Winnie-the-Pooh.

Charles Henry Harrod had a wholesale food and tea business in Stepney, East London, when he moved into a small shop in Knights-bridge in order to take advantage of the Great Exhibition crowds spilling into nearby Hyde Park in 1851. The business grew, but it was Harrod's son, also named Charles, who expanded the store's offerings to perfume, stationery, and medicine. By 1880, the shop employed a hundred people, but it burned down in 1883. Amazingly the store was up and running again in less than a year.

The massive store as it appears today was designed by C.W. Ste-phens, who also built Claridge's Hotel, and was constructed in stages between 1894 and 1912. The exterior is covered in terracotta fired by

Royal Doulton (which also produced the tiling in the food hall), Art Nouveau-inspired windows, and cherubs. The world's first escalator was installed here in 1898; brandy was offered at the end of the ride to settle the nerves. In the twentieth century, Harrod's established its own funeral services (Sigmund Freud was embalmed here), housed a lending library, and today sells airplanes and real estate.

The food hall is a haven for American expats longing for "exotic" ingredients like marshmallow fluff and Oreos, it also boasts some of the most beautiful displays in the store. The kitchenware department is overflowing—from the most basic vegetable peeler to the Lamborghini of espresso machines. Harrod's house label fashions for men and women offer fine cashmere sweaters, well-tailored shirts, and sleepwear.

While it remains a major tourist attraction, at over 1 million square feet, Harrod's can be overwhelming. Still, it's quite a sight.

Heal's

———— ◆ ————

EST. 1810

196 TOTTENHAM COURT ROAD, W1

☎ 020 7636 1666   ⊖ GOODGE STREET

www.heals.co.uk

MONDAY TO WEDNESDAY 10AM TO 6PM; THURSDAY 10AM TO
8PM; FRIDAY 10AM TO 6:30PM; SATURDAY 9:30AM TO 6:30PM;
SUNDAY NOON TO 6PM

IT IS HARD TO BELIEVE THAT TOTTENHAM COURT ROAD, TODAY LINED WITH CHEAP ELECTRONICS SHOPS, WAS ONCE the center of London's fine furniture business. In the nineteenth century it was known for its cabinetmakers, but by the Victorian era Tottenham Court Road was the center of the fine furniture-making trade. High end furniture was at its most lavish and expensive here by the mid-to-late 1800s, and the Chippendale and Heppelwhite workshops made it their home.

John Harris Heal opened a shop in nearby Rathbone Place in 1810 and moved to the large premises on Tottenham Court Road thirty years later. Heal's furniture-designer son, Ambrose, carried on the business and was in major part responsible for the steady ascent of the Arts and Crafts movement in Britain. "Modern and distinct" pieces of furniture are what made Heal's name.

Between 1912 and 1916, Ambrose's cousin Cecil Brewer designed a

new store beside their Victorian shopfront. By the standards of the day, it was the most modern and by far the largest store dedicated to the furniture and fittings trade. Heal's was also home to The Mansard Gallery, dedicated to the annual design exhibition entitled "Modern Tendencies in Furniture and Decoration."

Today the store still cuts a dash. On the exterior hangs a series of blue-enamel and cast-iron plaques depicting the heraldic symbols of the furniture trade. Inside, a fully stocked kitchenware department sits beside a enormous selection of tableware and a room full of picture frames. Upstairs, its legacy in the furniture trade is still going strong. Limited edition pieces from young British makers sit comfortably beside classics of modern design, and contemporary lines like Ligne Roset. On the ground floor, British chef Oliver Peyton has opened a small bakery serving sweet and savory items to take home.

Labour and Wait

EST. 2001

18 CHESHIRE STREET, E2

☎ 020 7729 6253   ⊖ LIVERPOOL STREET

www.labourandwait.co.uk

CLOSED MONDAY TO THURSDAY; FRIDAY OPEN BY
APPOINTMENT; SATURDAY 1PM TO 5PM; SUNDAY 10AM TO 5PM

JUST OFF TEEMING BRICK LANE, THE POPULAR LABOUR AND WAIT IS AT ONCE COMPLETELY AT HOME AND AN ANOMALY in this fad-driven part of London. Owners Simon Watkins and Rachel Wythe-Moran met while working in the men's fashion business but began turning their attention toward "proper things"—household and gardening items, especially—that weren't over-designed or über-trendy. They imagined a shop full of useful products sourced mainly from Britain that were design classics at their most fundamental: balls of twine with beautiful wrapping, enamel milk pans, old brown Lovatt's pottery, wooden children's toys, trowels, the perfect

LABOUR AND WAIT

1B CHESHIRE STREET · LONDON · E2 6EH

BROAD BEAN
PURPLE SEEDED

pencil, Penguin paperbacks. Their concept was a shop that was half Victorian garden shed and half postwar London kitchen.

The shop they created has followed that blueprint perfectly and been a brilliant success. Given the owners' antipathy to trendiness, it's ironic that Labour and Wait has become the darling of stylists and designers. The window display at Cheshire Street changes weekly and is always sublimely minimal, featuring three or four examples of a product or different products of the same color, in perfect alignment. Labour and Wait is the place to find all those things that seem to have disappeared forever. Note that there are small branches in Melrose and Morgan deli in Primrose Hill (see page 132) and in the Junya Watanabe concept store, Dover Street Market, in Mayfair.

Liberty

EST. 1875 ♛

GREAT MARLBOROUGH STREET AT REGENT STREET, W1

☎ 020 7734 1234   ⊖ OXFORD STREET

www.liberty.co.uk

MONDAY, TUESDAY, WEDNESDAY, FRIDAY 10AM TO 7PM;
THURSDAY 10AM TO 8PM; SATURDAY 10AM TO 7PM;
SUNDAY NOON TO 6PM

DESCRIBED AS AN "ENCHANTED CAVE" WHEN IT OPENED IN 1875, ARTHUR LIBERTY'S DEPARTMENT STORE REMAINS one of the quintessential shopping experiences in London.

Liberty was the son of a draper in Nottingham and had come to London eager to find work that suited his artistic nature. He joined Farmer & Rogers, a fashionable department store on Regent Street, in 1862, the year of the International Exhibition; it was the first year Japan had exhibited at a European event, and it made quite an impression on all who saw it. Farmer & Rogers purchased parts of the Japanese exhibits and had them reassembled in their shop as an "Oriental Warehouse," where they stocked silks, porcelains, lacquerware,

and other decorative items. Liberty became its manager and the Warehouse became something of a salon for the Pre-Rapaelites, who were fascinated by Asian craft and design; they soon befriended Liberty and invited him to their studios. After ten years at the Oriental Warehouse, Liberty asked to be made a partner in Farmer & Rogers; when he was denied the promotion he struck out on his own with the encouragement of some of his best customers.

He soon found a Regent Street bolthole of his own, which he christened—rather grandly—East India House. It was almost immediately a success, and within a few years London's appetite for artisan Japanese decorative objects was such that department stores throughout the city opened their own "Oriental" departments. (In the meantime, Farmer & Rogers shut down; the customers at Liberty's well-managed Oriental Warehouse all having jumped ship to patronize his new shop.)

Liberty soon began importing textiles, furniture, and objects from India, China, and the Middle East, and began dyeing and printing fabrics at Edmund Littler's block-printing works at the now-famous Merton Abbey in Surrey. He expanded into the building next door and opened a (short-lived) shop on avenue de l'Opéra in Paris in 1890. Thus began the unceasing demand for Liberty prints, miles of which were sold each week.

In the 1920s, Regent Street—created by architect John Nash to link the Prince Regent's residence to Regent's Park—was redesigned as a dedicated shopping street. Buildings facing Regent Street—owned by the Crown—had to fall into a prescribed planning regimen: Portland stone, classic lines and proportions, and, in Liberty's case, topped by an enormous frieze showing goods being transported from the East on elephants, camels, and ships. But Liberty had a long, ungainly site facing Great Marllborough Street, so in 1922–23 an elaborate scheme to build a Tudor-style shop was hatched and realized. Father and son architects Edwin and E. Stanley Hall were retained for the job. Central to their design was a frontage that appeared to be several small shops, an effect now somewhat lost. The teak and oak timbers used were salvaged from two British Man-of-War ships—the HMS *Hindustan* and the HMS *Impregnable* (the former, by amazing coinicidence, was the same length as the building's plot)—and properly mortised and pegged in the traditional way (as opposed to just stuck on for effect). The window glass was properly leaded, the stained glass panels made by respected firm Wainright & Waring, the roofing tiles hand-made. Inside, the dramatic atrium and four stories of galleried shopping nooks and crannies were floored in the deck timbers from the ships, the balustrades of the staircases were hand carved, and the overall effect was much more in tune with the "aesthetic" Liberty philosophy than the classical Regent Street frontage could ever have been.

Today, the allure remains. The store is uncompromisingly beautiful (and historically protected) and if Liberty prints aren't at the height of fashion these days, they are still available by the yard or made up into an endless variety of scarfs, bags, and other souvenirs. Liberty celebrates young British design and carries innovative lines by international fashion houses as well. There is a gallery that sells nineteenth-century Japanese woodblock prints and a section of the housewares department devoted to Art Deco and Arts and Crafts furnishings.

GROCERS & BUTCHERS

A. Gold

EST. 2000

42 BRUSHFIELD STREET, E1

☎ 020 7247 2487   ⊖ LIVERPOOL STREET

www.agold.co.uk

MONDAY TO FRIDAY 11AM TO 8PM; SATURDAY 10AM TO 6PM;
SUNDAY 11AM TO 6PM

IN THE SHADOW OF HAWKSMOOR'S MAGNIFICENT CHRIST CHURCH AND ACROSS THE STREET FROM A HULKING NEW office block, A. Gold grocers is in a short row of well-preserved and restored Georgian townhouses. Owners Safia and Ian Thomas have captured the soul of their shop and transformed it into the one they "always wanted to visit, but never found."

The shopfront belonged at one time to a Hungarian Jewish hatmaker, Amelia Gold, and the Thomases kept the name they uncovered on the storefront's façade. The street itself was cut in 1785, about the same time that the building and its neighbors were built.

123

Gold is the dream corner shop. In addition to the penny candy jars in the window that lure in lunchtime passers-by, the shop is stocked with all manner of fresh food and pantry items, all British and Irish (except the wine, which is French).

Homemade pies and a slicing ham share space on the marble countertop with wheels of myriad English cheeses, like Lancashire and mild Dorset goat, and smoked salmon. You can also buy organic eggs, drinking chocolate, and authentic Welsh cakes.

Allen & Co.

117 MOUNT STREET, W1

☎ 020 7499 5831 ⊖ BOND STREET

MONDAY TO FRIDAY 3:30AM TO 4PM;

SATURDAY 3:30AM TO NOON; CLOSED SUNDAY

THIS NEIGHBORHOOD BUTCHER PAR EXCELLENCE HAS BEEN A MAYFAIR STANDBY SINCE THE LATE NINETEENTH CENTURY. The shop occupies the corner ground floor of an 1887 building by James Trant Smith, part of a vast estate developed by the Duke of Westminster. The terracotta and red brick buildings around Mount Street—a melange of architectural styles that architectural

historian Nikolaus Pevsner called Franco-Flemish-Renaissance—are unique to Mayfair and lend the streets its unique color. Allen's façade (kitty-corner from the lovely and discreet Connaught Hotel) was described by the Duke as "overdone and wanting in simplicity." The original butcher, Edgar Green, gave way to Allen and Co. (which had already been established elsewhere in Mayfair) in the 1890s.

A worn, octagonal butcher-block

dominates the shop, and ceiling racks lag under sides of meat ready to be cut for each customer. The ornate tiling is original. In addition to the usual things to be expected from a butcher, Allen's is also known for its fine seasonal game and for occasionally having gulls' eggs. At Christmas time the small shop is literally draped in fresh turkeys. Customers have their meat cut to order and pay at the wooden window till, beneath the hunting trophies.

Jones Dairy

EST. 1982

23 EZRA STREET, E2

☎ 020 7739 5372 ⊖ LIVERPOOL STREET

www.jonesdairy.co.uk

CLOSED MONDAY TO THURSDAY; FRIDAY, SATURDAY 9AM
TO 3PM; SUNDAY 8AM TO 3PM

TRADITIONALLY, WELSH HILL FARMERS WOULD DRIVE THEIR LIVESTOCK EACH YEAR TO THE MARKETS IN LONDON and, further afield, to Kent. In the early 1900s, many moved to London permanently and established neighborhood dairies. Built in 1902, Jones Dairy is one such Welsh dairy shop. (The space that is today the Jones

Café, around the corner from the main shop, once housed eight cows that provided fresh milk to local residents.) Closed for many years, Jones Dairy was given new life in 1982, and is now one of the finest independent cheese shops in the city; it is certainly among the most redolent of a bygone age. Despite its name, Jones carries no milk—cheese is the draw here. There are usually a dozen or more British and Dutch cheeses (both pasteurized and

unpasteurized) on the counters, along with a mighty selection of bread from local, independent bakeries. The wooden shelves encircling the shop floor heave with organic nuts, preserves, teas, flours, apple juice, and a small selection of produce sits under the window in baskets.

Jones Dairy's distinctive four-piece blue sign (visible only when the shop is closed) double as window shutters, virtually unchanged from archival photos of the original shop. Note that breakfast and lunch are served in the café, which has outdoor seating on the cobbled walk connecting Ezra Street and Columbia Road. A perfect stop on a visit to the Sunday Flower Market, when freshly shucked oysters are also available from a stand beside the café.

TODAY'S ~
~ SPECIAL:

organic White bean &
chard Soup with roasted
pepper rouille

GREEN SALAD
MIXED SALAD

KIPPERS WITH BROWN BREAD

Mushrooms on toast
and Poached egg

HOMEMADE CAKES

PIZZA & SIDE SALAD

CARROT CAKE
Chocolate Brownies
CINNAMON BUNS
Welsh Fruit Cakes
Cheese Cake !!

Lina Stores

EST. 1930s

18 BREWER STREET, W1

☎ 020 7437 6482   ⊖ PICCADILLY CIRCUS

MONDAY TO FRIDAY 9AM TO 6:30PM; SATURDAY 9AM TO 5:30PM;

CLOSED SUNDAY

LINA'S PISTACHIO-GREEN INTERIOR IS WARM AND WELCOM-ING. THIS ITALIAN FOOD SHOP HAS BEEN RUN BY THE Filipis since 1975, when they bought it from the Lina family, who opened it in the 1930s. Its fresh ravioli, made on the premises daily, is sold straight from the stack on the counter, and its famous homemade sausages hang in strings above. Cubbyholes behind the store-length counter hold tins of beans, bags of flour, dry pasta, ground espresso, and polenta. Fresh bread, herbs, and sacks of dried beans fill out the space. Nearly any ingredient one might need is stashed somewhere here.

The modest corner exterior is original vitrolite and ceramic, and the glass signage evokes an earlier time in Soho's history, when Italian was commonly heard on the street and the legions of Swiss-Italians who had migrated early in the century to open restaurants were joined by others opening shops and cafés in Soho's buzzing streets.

Melrose and Morgan

EST. 2005

42 GLOUCESTER AVENUE, NW1

☎ 020 7722 0011   ⊖ CHALK FARM

www.melroseandmorgan.com

CLOSED MONDAY; TUESDAY TO FRIDAY 8AM TO 8PM;

SATURDAY 8AM TO 6PM; SUNDAY 10AM TO 6PM

NICK SELBY AND IAN JAMES OPENED THEIR DELI ON RESIDENTIAL GLOUCESTER AVENUE ONLY RECENTLY, BUT even a quick visit makes clear how deeply English tradition informs what they do.

Melrose and Morgan is simple and seductive. Two plate-glass cubes extend out into the sidewalk. One frames a grocery, which specializes in goods from throughout Britain; the other frames an open kitchen, which prepares food all day. Inside, the spaces are linked by a long farmhouse table topped with the bounty of the kitchen—savory tarts, cold salads, a slicing ham—and local baked goods. A glass-doored, walk-in refrigerator holds fresh soups, dairy goods, and supplies for the in-house kitchen, but everything is for sale. Need a soup bone? There may be one to be had. As Selby said in an

interview, "It feels like you're shopping in somebody else's kitchen."

Melrose and Morgan also sell a selection of kitchenware from Labour and Wait (see page 112), and they prepare lovely picnics to take to nearby Primrose Hill and dinners to feed a crowd to be delivered home. They also offer a monthly cooking school—call for details.

Verde & Co.

EST. 2004

40 BRUSHFIELD STREET, E1

☏ 020 7247 1924 ⊖ LIVERPOOL STREET

DAILY 8AM TO 8PM

WHEN WRITER JEANETTE WINTERSON BOUGHT HER GEORGIAN HOME IN SPITALFIELDS A FEW YEARS AGO, the ground floor fruiterer's shop had long been abandoned. In 2004, she had its original signage and interior handsomely restored and made it into a grocery once again. The shop's Continental leanings complement its next-door neighbor A. Gold (see page 123). Crates of apples, baskets of baby carrots, and jelly jars of flowers adorn the black-painted shop front, where you can also stop in for an espresso. A few tables are tucked into the interior. Former St. John (see page 248) chef Harvey Cabaniss manages the shop, sourcing his ingredients locally and sustainably. The dry goods lining the shelves include exquisitely packaged Japanese tea, Leone pastilles from Turin, and chutneys made in London's neighboring Home Counties. A glass case holds a rotating selection of Pierre Macollini chocolates.

Every few Fridays, Cabaniss serves homemade lunches and dinners, but seating is limited, so call in advance for details.

THE BUTTON QUEEN
LONDON

Coachman's Button from
State Livery to King
Edward VII.

NOTIONS SHOPS

HORN
TOGGLES
LARGE
£5.95
SMALL
£4.55

Button Queen

EST. 1968

19 MARYLEBONE LANE, W1

☎ 020 7935 1505   ⊖ BOND STREET

www.thebuttonqueen.co.uk

MONDAY, TUESDAY, WEDNESDAY 10AM TO 5PM; THURSDAY,
FRIDAY 10AM TO 6PM; SATURDAY 10AM TO 4PM;
CLOSED SUNDAY

THIS CLOSET-SIZED MARYLEBONE SHOP SPECIALIZES IN BUTTONS OF ALL KINDS. BUT WHAT WORLDS IT CONtains! It's easy to get lost among the bowls, jars, bags, trays, and boxes containing any color, size, or shape of button, frog, or stud. There are

thousands of run-of-the-mill mother-of-pearl buttons to choose from, in a variety of colors, but finding the unusual here is not difficult: fantastical Bimini glass buttons, kilt fasteners, Art Deco plastic and bakelite buttons can all be had. If it's possible that something you're looking for is not on the shop floor, all you need do is ask—if the store is not too busy, someone will happily check the treacherously stacked shelves in the back of the shop.

V.V. Rouleaux

EST. 1990

6 MARYLEBONE HIGH STREET, W1

☎ 020 7224 5179 ⊖ BAKER STREET

www.vvrouleaux.com

MONDAY, TUESDAY, THURSDAY, FRIDAY 9:30AM TO 6PM;

WEDNESDAY 10:30AM TO 6PM; SATURDAY 9:30AM TO 6PM;

CLOSED SUNDAY

ESTABLISHED IN 1990 BY ANNABEL LEWIS, A FORMER FLORIST, V.V. ROULEAUX (FOR "VERY VERY RIBBONS") HAS something of the floral still about it. Hundreds of rolls of ribbons in every color imaginable unfurl from a dozen or so three-tiered metal racks—grosgrain of multiple stripes and widths, satins; wire-edged organza; velvets. There is an endless selection of new and antique ribbons. Scattered around the ground floor and downstairs are other, sometimes seasonal, decorative notions: braids, feathers, silk milliners' flowers, wreaths of beads, rolls of bugle beading. Popular not just with those with obsessive gift-wrapping tendencies, fashion designers—from students to Paul Smith (see page 70)—and interior dec-

orators frequent the shop for inspiration and decorative flourish.

The Marylebone store opened in 1999 in a former butcher shop; the intricate tile work on the walls and floors is intact. Branches have since been opened in Newcastle and Glasgow, and London boasts a shop in Chelsea and the firm's headquarters, known as the Trade Vaults, in Battersea. Rugs with designs based on ribbon patterns and embellished furniture are also sold.

PUVEYORS OF SPECIALTY FOODS

Berry Bros. & Rudd

EST. 1698 ♛♛♛

3 ST. JAMES'S STREET, SW1

☎ 020 7396 9600   ⊖ GREEN PARK

www.bbr.com

MONDAY TO FRIDAY 10AM TO 6PM; SATURDAY 10AM TO 4PM;

CLOSED SUNDAY

A VERITABLE MUSEUM OF EIGHTEENTH-CENTURY TRADE, BERRY BROS. & RUDD IS BRITAIN'S OLDEST WINE MER-chant, having traded from the same shop for more than 300 years, and it's still a family-run enterprise. The building, which dates to the early seventeenth century, was once a coffee house known for being at "the sign of the coffee mill"—a sign which remains in place outside the shop to this day. Subsequently it was made into a grocers, and finally redeveloped in the 1730s to create the current shopfront.

The shop's main room is a paneled salon where customers can get advice on what employees here call the client's "wine needs." There is almost no wine is sight, except a few dusty bottles above the mantle and some impressive vintages in a locked glass-doored cupboard. Tables and antique Windsor chairs are scattered about the rough-hewn floor, and an enormous scale dominates the rear of the shop; a fixture since 1765, it was originally used for weighing sacks of coffee. But over the years it has weighed visitors including Byron, Napoleon III, and Vivien Leigh. Those who want to add their names to a list of those whose weights have been recorded in the ledgers can do so if they call ahead. Toward the back of the store is an oak-lined parlor, where for many years the directors had their lunch together every day and where, in 1923, Francis Berry and James McBey decided to make and market a new blend of whiskey: Cutty Sark.

The shop's double cellars are said to hold 100,000 bottles of wine. The lower, brick-vaulted Napoleon Cellar doubles as a dining room that can be reserved for parties and events. A photographic history of the firm lines the stairwell connecting it to the Pickering Cellar, where tastings are held—and where a doorway, long since bricked up, is believed to have led to a passage connecting the cellars to St. James's Palace.

Recently, Berry Bros. has opened a new section of the shop, next door at number 2, where those who already know their "wine needs" can buy a bottle or two in a bright, modern shop. Berry Bros. holds two Royal Warrants and it has been keeping the royal family in wine since George III. French wine remains a specialty, but a selection of unusual sprits and fine cognacs is also available, along with single malt whiskeys made under the Berry Bros. & Rudd label.

A curious bit of history connects the building with America. It was here that the government of Texas, when still an independent country, set up its embassy from 1845 to 1852. There is a commemorative plaque in the alleyway leading from St. James's Street to Pickering Place.

Brick Lane Beigel Bake

EST. 1855

159 BRICK LANE, E1

☎ 020 7729 0616 ⬤ LIVERPOOL STREET

DAILY 24 HOURS

THE BEIGEL BAKE IS AN EAST END INSTITUTION. IT'S ALWAYS OPEN (A RARITY IN LONDON) AND ALWAYS BUSY; there's almost always a taxi driver being served alongside a police officer and a transvestite club kid.

But the bakery was here long before the clubs moved into Brick Lane, before the moniker "Banglatown" was bandied about by real estate developers. The bakery began in the middle of the nineteenth century, when Whitechapel was the heart of the robust Jewish East End. Eastern European Jews fled the pogroms to London and set up as butchers, cabinet makers, tailors, and bakers. What is today a mosque down the street was the synagogue; the first Yiddish Theatre in England opened in 1886 about five blocks away. Today the Beigel Bake sits contentedly between

BEIGELS

½	Dz	0.90
1	Dz	1.80
1.½	Dz	2.70
2	Dz	3.60
2.½	Dz	4.50
3	Dz	5.40
3.½	Dz	6.30
4	Dz	7.20
4.½	Dz	8.10
5	Dz	9.00
5.½	Dz	9.90
6	Dz	10.80
6.½	Dz	11.70
7	Dz	12.60

8	Dz	14.40
8.½	Dz	15.30
9	Dz	16.20
9.½	Dz	17.10
10	Dz	18.00
10.½	Dz	18.90
11	Dz	19.8
11.½	Dz	20.7
12	Dz	21.6
12.½	Dz	22.
13	Dz	23.
13.½	Dz	24
14	Dz	2

the nearby "Soup Kitchen for the Jewish Poor," which has been transformed into luxury apartments, and the curry houses of Brick Lane.

For many years bagels were the only baked good on offer—and cream cheese and smoked salmon were the only choice of accompaniments. Today you can get challa, platzels (a cross between a roll and a bialy) cheesecake, and decent salt beef (corned beef) on a bagel for just £2.30.

Charbonnel et Walker

EST. 1875 ♔♔♔

1 ROYAL ARCADE, W1

☎ 020 7491 0939   ⊖ PICCADILLY CIRCUS

www.charbonnel.co.uk

MONDAY TO FRIDAY 10AM TO 6PM; SATURDAY 10AM TO 5PM;

CLOSED SUNDAY

IN 1873, THE (SOON-TO-BE EDWARD VIII) ENCOURAGED MADAME CHARBONNEL OF MAISON BOISSER CHOCOLATIER IN Paris to come to London and join forces with English confectioner Mrs. Walker to make chocolate: so began one of the first chocolate producers in England. The women later opened a shop on Bond Street, which remained in business for nearly a century before moving to the Royal Arcade in the 1970s, when it received a Royal Warrant from the Queen.

Charbonnel et Walker's drinking chocolate is probably the firm's most recognizable product. Sold in a black and white tin that looks like a relic of the Victorian age, its prevalence in London somewhat overshadows the lovely confections and beautifully packaged treats also available at the Royal Arcade boutique. Their champagne-infused truffles can be bought in pretty round boxes that resemble old-fashioned face powder containers or you can make your own selection from violet and rose creams, noisettes, marzipans, and caramels, which will be packed in an elegant blue-trimmed box.

KNIFE THRU HEAD

Hope and Greenwood

EST. 2004

20 NORTH CROSS STREET, SE 22

www.hopeandgreenwood.co.uk

☎ 020 8613 1777 ⊖ EAST DULWICH RAIL

MONDAY TO SATURDAY 10AM TO 6PM; SUNDAY 10AM TO 5PM

A FEW BLOCKS UPHILL FROM EAST DULWICH'S POPULAR THOROUGHFARE LORDSHIP LANE (SEE FRANKLIN'S; PAGE 220), Hope and Greenwood is a sugar haven, redolent of an English postwar penny candy shop: pink and red with a bench outside; curtains and boxes of chocolates in the window; shelves overflowing with 185 jars of confections customers probably think are no longer made (many of which will probably be unfamiliar to non-British customers), along with Hope and Greenwood's homemade chocolates.

One of the owners, who goes only by Miss Hope, enjoys playing the part of a '50s shopkeeper. She can be found leaning over the marble topped counter—trying to quell the delirium

of a group of overexcited children—looking straight out of a 1950s advertisement: her period up do, cherry red lips, flowered pinnie, and heels set the tone for the spirit of the shop. In keeping with the postwar decor and theme, the shop issues a "ration book" for parents to give their children for a "daily ration."

Behind the marble counter and lining the walls are hundreds of jars of candy—Fat Lips, Milk Bottles, White Mice, Sherbert Lemons, Cola Cubes, and two dozen kinds of licorice. Customers can also pick up a basket at the entrance and fill it from the boxes and jars set out on the vintage cupboards, to be counted and weighed at the counter.

Maison Bertaux

EST. 1871

28 GREEK STREET, W1

☎ 020 7437 6007 ⊖ LEICESTER SQUARE

MONDAY TO SATURDAY 8:30AM TO 11PM; CLOSED SUNDAY

A SLICE OF PARIS IN LONDON, THIS FRENCH PATISSERIE CLAIMS TO BE THE OLDEST CAFÉ IN SOHO. IT IS CERtainly one of the few with any character left in the neighborhood, and offers what may be the best croissants in town. The space can barely contain the cases of *patisserie*, a few tables, and an upright piano, and the tempting smell of sugar and pastry wafts outside. The upstairs room is decorated with pink netting and beads and a few wooden seats and tables, and there is a black-and-white photo above the mantle showing the original shop and its bakers and waiters. Customers can take out fine Paris

Brest, pretty *milles feuilles*, and *petits fours* or eat in and have *croques* and pastries and tea, but best is whatever has been just prepared. There are few better places in central London when the weather is rainy and cold, and the service is charming—as long as you don't ask for a menu, because there isn't one.

On some evenings the twenty seats upstairs become part of what must be London's smallest theater, as impromptu plays are staged starring one or two of the wait staff (who moonlight as actors) or the sisters who run the café. There is a also an annual staff re-enactment of the storming of the Bastille each July 14th.

Marine Ices

EST. 1931

8 HAVERSTOCK HILL, NW3

☎ 0871 332 1192   ⊖ CHALK FARM

www.marineices.co.uk

MONDAY TO FRIDAY NOON TO 3PM; 6PM TO 11PM;

SATURDAY NOON TO 11PM; SUNDAY NOON TO 10PM

O N BALMY SUMMER DAYS THE LINE AT MARINE ICE'S GELATO WINDOW STRETCHES DOWN THE HILL TOWARD Camden and is a regular stop for those returning from Hampstead Heath or Primrose Hill.

When founder Gaetano Mansi emigrated to London he opened a fruit stand; out of the daily left overs he made sorbet and gelato that he sold to his regular customers. It wasn't long before these became known to restauranteurs and hoteliers, and the ice creams and sorbets from "Casa Mansi" became his full-time endeavor. Now run by third generation Mansi family members, the first-

rate gelato and sorbet are made in the mini-factory upstairs, which can produce seven-hundred quarts a day. They can be bought by the cone or the quart from the window on the street.

There is also a roomy, family-friendly restaurant, don't let the bright green walls and matching chairs put you off. The Mansis serve terrific pizzas and above average pasta dishes at reasonable prices, and all the bread and sausage is made fresh on the premises. The gelateria at the back also has a seating area.

Neal's Yard Dairy

EST. 1979

17 SHORTS GARDENS, WC2

☎ 020 7240 5700   ⊖ COVENT GARDEN

www.nealsyarddairy.co.uk

MONDAY TO THURSDAY 11AM TO 6:30PM; FRIDAY 10AM TO
6:30PM; SATURDAY 10AM TO 6:30PM; CLOSED SUNDAY

"**F**ARM CHEESES AND PRODUCE FROM THE BRITISH ISLES":
SIMPLE AS THAT. THE SPARE SPACE THAT NEAL'S YARD
occupies, nearly every inch filled with cheese, was founded by Nicholas Saunders in 1979. (He also launched the Monmouth Coffee shop in Covent Garden.) After a year of selling only fresh cheeses and yogurts made on the premises, Randolph Hodgson, who had helped set up the

shop, took over and began sourcing farmhouse cheeses from around Great Britain, after a Devon-based cheesemaker sent Hodgson a sample of her cheese. Hodgson became devoted to educating himself about the culture of cheesemaking in the British Isles—and bringing it to the growing ranks of customers at Neal's Yard.

Neal's Yard cheeses are jabbed

FEATURE CHEESES

APPLEBY'S CHESHIRE

HARD COW'S MILK CHEESE MADE
AT ABBEY FARM, WHITCHURCH
UNPASTEURISED COW'S MILK.
VEG RENNET £16.50/KG

ST GALL

HARD COW'S MILK CHEESE
MADE IN C° CORK, IRELAND.
UNPASTEURISED COW'S MILK
TRAD. RENNET £20.60/KG

with incredibly detailed signs specifying the names of the cheesemaker, the kind of milk used, the location of the farm, the age of the cheese ... everything but the names of the goats and cows (and sometimes even that!). Customers are encouraged to taste cheeses before buying, a wonderful treat—though it can be a test of patience at Christmas time, when lines can stretch down the street. Still, seeing chunks of traditional Stilton and Lancashire cut straight from huge wheels is great fun.

The cheesemaking operation has been moved off site to Herefordshire, where Neal's Yard Creamery supplies the shops with a sweet crème fraîche, goat's curd, and yogurt. They have also opened a shop on Park Street behind Borough Market (see page 283), near where the company has also built a warehouse and cheese-aging cave into the arches beneath the rail bridges in Southwark.

TARTARE
SAUCE

THE PERFECT
ACCOMPANIMENT
FOR FISH
DISHES

MANGO
CHUTNEY

AUTHENTIC
INDIAN
FLAVOURS.
SERVE WITH
CURRIES OR
COLD MEATS.

PICCA-
LILLI

AN ENGLISH
RECIPE MADE
WITH FRESH
VEGETABLES.
DELICIOUS WITH
COLD MEATS OR CHEESE

OLD ENG
TANGY PI
WITH REAL A

SWEETLY PI
FRUIT & VEG
GREAT WI
MEAT PIE

FARM-
HOUSE
PICKLE

PERFECT
PARTNER FOR
A PLOUGHMAN'S
PLATTER

CRANBERRY
SAUCE

MADE WITH
WHOLE FRESH
FRUITS - A
MUST WITH
TURKEY

POACHER'S
PICKLE

FRUITY AND
DELICIOUS
PERFECT WITH
GAME PIES
SMOKED MEATS
& MATURE CHEESE

Paul Rothe & Son

EST. 1900

35 MARYLEBONE LANE, W1

☎ 020 7935 6783 ⊖ BOND STREET

MONDAY TO FRIDAY 8AM TO 6PM; SATURDAY 11:30AM TO

5:30PM; CLOSED SUNDAY

PAUL ROTHE & SON IS A LONDON CURIOSITY—THE CLOSEST THING TO A NEW YORK-STYLE DELI ONE MIGHT FIND here. Paul Rothe opened his shop in the winding Marylebone Lane when he emigrated from Germany in 1900. Naturalized in 1906, he was called up to serve during World War I, and his wife ran the shop until he returned. In 1940, his son Robert took over the shop. Shelves hold jams, chutneys, and biscuits and a long deli counter is filled with cheeses and meats, salads, and appetizers. There are also homemade soups and pies. At the turn of the 1950s, when supermarkets put many small food shops out of business, Rothe became more of a café than strictly a deli; in went Formica tables and leatherette stools and chairs so that the homemade lunches could be enjoyed in the shop. Robert Rothe's son is now the proprietor.

Paxton & Whitfield

EST. 1797 〰〰

93 JERMYN STREET, SW1

☎ 020 7930 0259   ⊖ GREEN PARK

www.paxtonandwhitfield.co.uk

MONDAY TO SATURDAY 9:30AM TO 6PM; CLOSED SUNDAY

Immortalized in Eric Ravilious' 1938 "High Street" paintings and heralded by Winston Churchill as the only place "a gentleman" would buy his cheese, this is one of the finest cheesemongers in the city. Indeed, it's one of the finest shops of any kind in London. Ian Nairn, the unparalleled London townscape observer and critic, included it in the 1966 edition of his classic book, *Nairn's London*—the only shop he included. This longstanding "Cheesemongers by Appointment" deserves the praise and has held a Royal Warrant since 1870.

Paxton & Whitfield didn't trade under its current name until 1837. It modest beginnings were in Clare Market (near what is today Kingsway in Holborn) where Suffolk-native Stephen Cullum opened a shop in 1740 and led his son Sam into the business. With a partner, someone with a business in fancy provisions and connections to the royal household, Sam Cullum began specializing in the finest cheeses, those requested by the Prince Regent and the aristocracy, and took on a young man named Harry Paxton. Cullum soon bought out a friend's provisions business—the friend was named Whitfield. When Cullum retired he handed his share over to Harry Paxton's son, and soon Paxton & Whitfield was born.

These convolutions belie a simple mission: to sell the finest farmhouse and imported cheeses in London. In the present premises since 1896, the building, built in 1674, remains virtually unchanged. The deep shop has a narrow space for customers between the tempting counter piled with enormous rounds of cheese and the shelves of biscuits, chut-

neys, and other dry goods. Today they specialize in British and French cheeses. Their offerings range from the pungent "Oxford Isis," a domestic semi-soft cheese washed in honey-flavored mead to a fine AOC vacherin called "Mont d'Or" from the Jura mountains and wrapped in spruce bark. Books about cheese, various slate and wood cheeseboards, and a wide assortment of cheese knives are also for sale.

Prestat

EST. 1902 ♛

14 PRINCES ARCADE, SW1

☎ 020 7629 4838   ⊖ PICCADILLY CIRCUS

www.prestat.co.uk

MONDAY TO FRIDAY 9AM TO 6PM; SATURDAY 9AM TO 5PM;

CLOSED SUNDAY

PRINCES ARCADE, ERECTED AROUND 1930, WAS THE LAST COVERED SHOPPING ARCADE BUILT IN LONDON. IT LACKS the architectural and historical majesty of earlier arcades, and has the samey-same quality of most shopping malls. But it does boast Prestat, a Royal Warranted chocolatier. It was established in 1902 by French émigré

Antoine Dufour, who was Napoleon III's chocolatier and whose family had invented the chocolate truffle in 1895. When he came to London, he brought with him the recipes that had made him famous in the French court.

The tiny Princes Arcade corner shop can barely accommodate more than two customers at a time, but the air is thick with

the aroma of chocolate and the shelves are heaving with their brightly colored, gold-lettered packaging. Their chocolate-dipped apricots are superb. Roald Dahl fans may recognize the name Prestat from *My Uncle Oswald*, in which Prestat chocolates take a leading role.

W. Martyn

EST. 1897

135 MUSWELL HILL BROADWAY, N10

☎ 020 8883 5642 ⊖ HIGHGATE · *www.wmartyn.co.uk*

MONDAY TO WEDNESDAY 9:30AM TO 5:30PM; THURSDAY 9:30AM
TO 1PM; FRIDAY 9:30AM TO 5:30PM; SATURDAY 9AM TO 5:30PM;
CLOSED SUNDAY

LEAFY MUSWELL HILL HAS VIEWS OF THE THAMES AND LEA RIVER VALLEYS THAT MAKE THE NOT-SO-DISTANT CITY seem almost tranquil. While the march of modernization hasn't spared this once remote suburb, its High Street still boasts traditional and family owned shops.

W. Martyn's black, Art Deco façade and red signage stands out among these. It is a popular grocer among locals, who call it the Fortnum & Mason of Muswell Hill. It is owned and managed today by the founder's great-grandson, William Martyn, who is often in the store with his young son. Bags of coffee beans and an old coffee roaster sit in the window of the shop, providing locals and restaurants in central London with coffee from a long list of offerings. Originally more of a general store, a brass scale on the counter is still used to weigh out sugar and nuts, which are sold from sacks behind the counter. Coffee takes precedence today, along with the loose tea, bagged spices, jams and mustards, and organic flours in display cases mounted on original oak "barley-twist" columns.

TOBACCONISTS

G. SMITH & SONS
BOLIVAR
CORONAS
£9.70 EACH
£232.00 PER BOX OF 25

G. Smith and Sons

EST. 1869

74 CHARING CROSS ROAD, WC2

☎ 020 7836 7422　⊖ LEICESTER SQUARE

MONDAY TO FRIDAY 9AM TO 7:30PM;

SATURDAY 9:30AM TO 8PM; CLOSED SUNDAY

THE FADING BLUE FAÇADE OF SMITH'S ALMOST DISAPPEARS INTO ITS GRUBBY SURROUNDINGS OF CHARING CROSS' bookshops, West End theaters, and Chinese groceries. Its location makes it a popular haunt of theatergoers, who along with the countless passing tourists keep it in business. The modest glass signage above the entrance dates to the nineteenth century; the antique display cabinets inside hold pipes, and stacks of drawers contain overstock of snuff and tobacco. The little Highland figure standing sentry in the shop is the traditional eighteenth-century British version of the cigar store Indian. In addition to cigarettes, pipe tobacco, and cigars, Smith's does a good trade in pipes and accessories.

James J. Fox and Robert Lewis

EST. 1787 ♛

19 ST. JAMES'S STREET, SW1

☎ 020 7930 3787   ⊖ GREEN PARK

www.jjfox.co.uk

MONDAY TO SATURDAY 9AM TO 6PM; CLOSED SUNDAY

AMID THE COUNTLESS MEMBER'S CLUBS IN ST. JAMES'S IS WHAT—IN THE MINDS OF MANY CIGAR AFICIONADOS— is something of a club in itself: James J. Fox and Robert Lewis is the oldest specialty cigar and tobacco shop in England and, by its reckoning, perhaps the world. Christopher Lewis established his business, in Covent Garden, in 1787. Fox and his heirs started out as tobacco traders

in Dublin in the late nineteenth century before setting up a tobacco importing company and finally a tobacco shop in London's Burlington Gardens in 1946. A Lewis relation, Robert, was the first to import Cuban cigars to London. These two longstanding tobacco and cigar specialty stores formed a union in 1992.

The parlor-like shop dates

from 1834. Two cigar store Indians imported from America stand guard outside. Inside, cigars are laid out like museum pieces in glass-topped oak cases, and the use of storage humidors is offered for regular clients. The creaking plank floors and mahogany cases hold an encyclopedic selection of tobacco and cigar accoutrements, with one entire wall lined with hundreds of pipes. Under a palm tree in a cozy corner there are a few chairs for customers to relax. One of them is said to have been Churchill's preferred spot when he shopped here, and at the back of the shop is the Fox Museum, where one can see an unfinished box of his favorite Havanas.

ROMEO Y JULIETA
25 PETIT CORONAS
ROMEO Y JULIETA
25 PETIT CORONAS
25 Cedros de Luxe No. 3
ROMEO Y JULIETA
25 Cedros de Luxe No. 3
ROMEO Y JULIETA
25 Cedros de Luxe No. 2
ROMEO Y JULIETA

UMBRELLA SHOPS

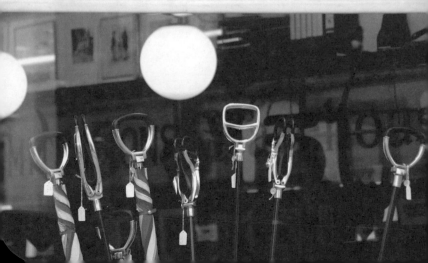

James Smith and Sons

EST. 1830 🦁

53 NEW OXFORD STREET, WC1

☎ 020 7836 4731   ⊖ HOLBORN

www.james-smith.co.uk

MONDAY TO FRIDAY 9:30AM TO 5:25PM;

SATURDAY 10AM TO 5:25PM; CLOSED SUNDAY

THIS QUINTESSENTIAL LONDON SHOP IS WEDGED BETWEEN THE MUNDANITY OF HIGH STREET RETAILERS AND THE majesty of the British Museum. Wooden cabinets and racks, custom fitted when the shop opened in 1857, overflow with handmade umbrellas and walking sticks.

James Smith founded his business in the West End in 1830; his son moved the business to New Oxford Street a generation later. Descendants of the original Smiths still own and manage the business. The original Victorian shopfront remains almost completely intact: reverse gilded and painted glass, painted glass panels, engraved brass, and half-round timber are in exquisite condition.

James Smith umbrellas are built

using Fox frames (for Samuel Fox, inventor of the steel umbrella frame) and can be custom made. Customers can also choose from a wide range of unusual fabrics, patterns, and handles if purchasing off the rack. The firm also specializes in ceremonial umbrellas and maces, and, perhaps more practically, walking sticks. Smith was the original maker of the "Cunliffe Sports Seat," which was a walking stick that converted into a camp seat. They make similar models today for the less sporty.

The prices are high, but these umbrella will likely last a lifetime. Assistance is as thorough or hands-off as the customer prefers. The patient gentlemen staffing the shop are happy to root through drawers looking for just the right handle. They also do repairs.

T. Fox and Co.

EST. 1868

118 LONDON WALL, EC1

☎ 020 7628 1868 ⊖ MOORGATE

www.tfox.co.uk

MONDAY TO FRIDAY 9AM TO 6PM;

CLOSED SATURDAY AND SUNDAY

THIS CHARMING UMBRELLA SHOP (NO CONNECTION TO THE INVENTOR OF THE FOX STEEL UMBRELLA FRAME; SEE James Smith and Sons, page 185) is set in a lovely and unusual building. It commands a small plaza at the busy intersection of London Wall and Moorgate; the space was created by Second World War bomb damage, and much of the area was rebuilt. Fox and the adjacent buildings are the oldest survivors here (beside the fragments of the Roman wall visible farther up the street toward the Museum of the City of London). The elegant Art Deco shopfront was installed in 1937 using curving nonreflective glass (which makes it seem as though there is no glazing in the window at all), neon, glossy black virtolite, and "running" chrome foxes.

ET CETERA

Allodi Accordions

EST. 1981

143-145 LEE HIGH ROAD, SE13

☎ 020 8244 3771 ⊖ LEWISHAM DLR

www.accordians.co.uk

MONDAY 2PM TO 6PM; TUESDAY, THURSDAY,
FRIDAY 10:30AM TO 6PM; SATURDAY 10:30AM TO 6PM;
CLOSED SUNDAY

BRUNO ALLODI, AN ACCOMPLISHED PROFESSIONAL MUSI-CIAN, EMIGRATED WITH HIS WIFE AND SON TO LONDON from Parma in 1951. As a young man, Allodi apprenticed with Busilacchio, the leading accordion manufacturer in Italy and establish his own shop in North London in 1954. There he built, restored, and sold accordions, and gave lessons. He became a renowned maestro of the accordion, sought out by players and afficionados eveywhere. Bruno Allodi passed away in 2006, but the family's trade is being continued by one of his children, Emilio Allodi. He has carried on his father's tradition and trade and opened his Allodi accordian shop in Lewisham in 1981. Here, the sagging shelves are lined with accordions of all ages and types. Mr. Allodi happily shows customers around, demonstrating any instrument they might take an interest in. Allodi is virtually a museum of the accordion and an unusual shop in a part of London even most Londoners don't know—a dying breed.

Arthur Beale

EST. 1895

194 SHAFTESBURY AVENUE, WC2

☎ 020 7836 9034   ⊖ COVENT GARDEN

MONDAY TO FRIDAY 10AM TO 5:30PM;

SATURDAY 10:30AM TO 5:30PM; CLOSED SUNDAY

MAROONED BETWEEN THE TRENDY SAMENESS OF COVENT GARDEN AND THE CHAOTIC BUSTLE OF LONDON'S Chinatown, upper Shaftesbury Avenue is an unlikely location for this century-old ship chandlers. But having helped many of the local West End theatres with rigging over the years, Beale seems serendipitously placed

The teal shopfront matches the pegboards inside, festooned with gleaming brass shackles, bolts, and hooks of every size and description. Spools of ropes adorn all sides of the store and rigging is still assembled in a downstairs workshop. Beale's is a stunning shop, as much for its incongruity as for its dazzling display.

Benjamin Pollock's Toyshop

EST. 1988

44 THE MARKET, COVENT GARDEN, WC2

☎ 020 7379 7866 ⊖ COVENT GARDEN

www.pollocks-coventgarden.co.uk

MONDAY TO FRIDAY 10:30AM TO 6PM;

SATURDAY 10:30AM TO 6PM; SUNDAY 11AM TO 4PM

IN THE FORMER FLOWER HALL OF THE NOW-DEFUNCT COVENT GARDEN MARKET IS THE V&A'S FINE, BUT UNDER-rated, Theatre Museum, a nod to Covent Garden's long association with the London theater, placed as it is between the West End and the theaters emanating off the nearby Strand.

The two-room Benjamin Pollock's Toyshop sits atop one of the arcaded market buildings in The Piazza—architect Inigo Jones's tribute to the great Italian squares he visited in the sixteenth century. Up a spiraling staircase is a jumbled collection of delightful traditional toys for children, including zoetropes, hand puppets, and toy theaters along with miniature stage sets of particular plays that can be manipulated manually, usually made of card-stock but often found in more elaborate wooden versions, too.

Though open only since 1988, the eponymous Pollock was a popular dealer of toy theaters in East London in the mid- to late nineteenth century, when the huge success of the London theater spawned hundreds of tiny versions of popular plays and operas.

Pollock's legacy was—and likely would have remained—forgotten had a woman named Marguerite Fawdry not come across the neglected stock of Pollock's long closed East London shop in the 1960s. With the newly unearthed treasures, she opened a museum dedicated to toy theaters and other traditional toys in Fitzrovia, in 1969, which she called The Benjamin Pollock Toy Museum (it is located at 1 Scala Street, W1, a short walk from Goodge Street Station, near the Samuel French theatre bookshop; see page 35). The present store in Covent Garden is run by Peter Baldwin, a long-time admirer of and visitor to the museum. It stocks a wide array of modern and antique toy theaters, ranging from antique Italian-made tin stage sets for grand operas to new UK-made card-stock theaters, one featuring the set for Moliere's *Malade Imaginaire*, to an intricate model of Shakespeare's Globe. Marionettes, music boxes, nesting dolls, and period paper doll kits round out the stock. A must for adults and children.

Cutler and Gross

EST. 1971 🦁

7 AND 16 KNIGHTSBRIDGE GREEN, SW1

☎ 020 7590 9995   ⊖ KNIGHTSBRIDGE

www.cutlerandgross.co.uk

MONDAY 1PM TO 6PM; TUESDAY TO FRIDAY 11AM TO 6PM;

SATURDAY 11AM TO 6PM; CLOSED SUNDAY

GRAHAM CUTLER AND TONY GROSS HAVE BEEN MAKING SIGNATURE EYEWEAR IN ENGLAND FOR OVER THIRTY years. They create cutting-edge frames in lightweight metals, chunky plastic throwbacks to the 1950s and 1960s, and well-proportioned buffalo horn-rimmed frames. It may be a favorite of stylists and celebrities, but the shop is neither pretentious nor intimidating and there isn't a pair of glasses in stock that is wacky or unwearable. The voluble and cheerful Tony Gross is often on hand himself to give exams or offer advice.

The small Cutler and Gross shop, in a pedestrian passage near the Knightsbridge tube station, was designed by architect Piers Gough and overhauled by celebrated British designer Tom Bartlett. In 2001, the duo opened a vintage shop up the walk at number 7. It carries not only a selection of frames from the Cutler and Gross archive, but also pieces from Tony Gross's own collection of vintage frames.

James Purdey & Sons

EST. 1814 ♛ ♛ ♛

57-58 SOUTH AUDLEY STREET, W1

☎ 020 7499 1801 ⊖ BOND STREET

www.purdey.com

MONDAY TO FRIDAY 9:30AM TO 5:30PM;

SATURDAY 10AM TO 5PM; CLOSED SUNDAY

FOR THOSE WHO DON'T KNOW THE DIFFERENCE BETWEEN A MUZZLE-LOADING FLINTLOCK AND A BREECH-LOADING hammerless ejector, the clerks at Purdey are happy to explain; they have sold hunting rifles for nearly two centuries.

Founder James Purdey worked for gunmaker Joseph Manton before establishing his own gunsmith operation in 1826. His first royal patronage came twelve years later, when Queen Victoria bought two Purdey pistols (for what purpose, it is not known). But it wasn't until 1868 that the Prince of Wales (soon to be King Edward VII) granted his firm its first Warrant.

Though no longer owned by the Purdey family, the firm is still in Audley House, its longtime Mayfair premises designed by James Purdey Jr. Custom-made and stock rifles are sold here but manufactured at Purdey's Hammersmith factory. A custom-made rifle takes from eighteen to twenty-four months to make, depending on the customer's specifications. Purdey's stands alone in retaining a traditional apprenticeship program at the factory: apprentices (almost exclusively men) enter at age sixteen and emerge at twenty-one as a master gunmaker, permitted to engrave a maker's mark on each piece he creates.

Each gun starts with a wood blank; Purdey prefers Turkish walnut for its combination of light weight, strength, striking patterns, and colored finishes. Even those unaccustomed to guns can take pleasure in a visit to Purdey's Gun Room, where rifles are lined up in cases under hunting trophies.

It's not all barrels and muzzles here, though. A large selection of hunting clothes and accessories for both men and women is available, as well as fine leather goods, books, walking sticks, and umbrellas.

Witcomb Cycles

EST. 1949

25 TANNERS HILL, SE 8

☎ 020 8692 1734   ⊖ DEPTFORD BRIDGE DLR

www.witcombcycles.com

MONDAY, TUESDAY, WEDNESDAY, FRIDAY 9:30AM TO 5PM;

THURSDAY AND SATURDAY 9:30AM TO 4PM; CLOSED SUNDAY

THE DEEP FORD FROM WHICH DEPTFORD GETS ITS NAME HAS LONG SINCE DISAPPEARED, AND THE MANY DISCOUNT stores and kebab shops hide the storied past of this riverside village. In the early sixteenth century, Henry VIII established a naval yard here; it is where the ships that defeated the Spanish Armada in 1588 were built. As

Deptford industrialized, the wealthy families who had seen the village as an escape from the The Big Smoke began relocating to leafier neighborhoods to the south. The Deptford Power Station was built in 1889 to supply not the local community, but London's booming West End; it is now disused. Despite heavy Second World War bombing, Deptford remained a busy shipping industry port until the 1960s, but then suffered steep decline and urban blight.

YOU CANNOT GET BETTER THAN A HAND BUILT LWEIGHT MADE BY THE EXPERTS SINCE 1949

TALK TO BARRY NOW

YOU HAVE SEEN THE REST NOW HAVE THE BEST BUILT ON THE PREMISES

W...
FRAMESETS AND
...ES TO ORDER
...K FOR DETAILS OF
SPECIAL PRICES
2006.
... BARRY .... PREMISES ON THE

Despite bombs, falling fortunes, and concrete, a few early seventeenth-century timber-framed buildings in Deptford survived. The best of them are along the bend of Tanners Hill and have been used as shops since the nineteenth century; Witcomb Cycles (and its neighbor, the superbly named Wellbeloved Butchers, who sell well-beloved, homemade savory pies) are a small glimpse of Deptford's past.

Former greengrocer Ernie Witcomb and his son Barry are the proprietors of Witcomb Cycles. They build handsome bicycle frames by hand in the traditional way: using an open hearth over which to shape the metal. Emblazoned with a red and green "W" badge, their custommade frames are popular with racing cyclists and those with special needs; among other things, they've made bicycles for circus performers. The marquetry cashier's desk is littered with rubber stamps and receipt pads. Though officially retired, Ernie is often in the store and quick with answers, stories, and advice. Within moments it's evident his enthusiasm lives up to the shop's motto: "Witcomb's heart is a frame."

ICH DIEN

BY APPOINTMENT

The Royal Warrant

WHILE IT MAY BE DIFFICULT IMAGINING ANY MEMBER OF THE MONARCHY SHOPPING, THERE EXISTS A HOMERIC list of firms who have "written authority to supply goods" to the royal household. They are called "Royal Warrant holders" and when in London you may notice a royal seal for the Queen, Prince Charles, Prince Philip, or the late Queen Mother adorning a store's façade or shopping bags. Nominated by the members of the royal family for dedicated service after a period of five years, the Warrant is signed and approved by the Lord Chamberlain, secretary of the royal household in an act of "loyalty for loyalty." It is not just shops that are warranted. Along with the outfitters, gunmakers, and supermarkets preferred by the royal family, there are suppliers of everything from parasols to Christmas crackers. A Warrant granted by a deceased member of the royal family is only removed five years after his or her death; in addition Warrant holders are reviewed every five years.

The first known example of the royal family establishing a formal relationship with a tradesman was when Henry II gave the Weavers Company a Royal Charter to provide cloth to the royal household in 1155. Subsequently, the charter system changed from singling out a trade or service to singling out an individual of expert craftsmanship or trade. Today the Royal Warrant, even if supplied to a shop, is actually granted to an individual representing the company (usually a director). In 1476 a Warrant was granted to the first English printer, William Caxton. Henry

VIII appointed a Warrant to Thomas Hewytt to supply him with swans; Charles II's list of grantees in 1684 included a swordmaker and a golf club maker. William IV's household granted Warrants to a pin maker, a card maker, and a rat catcher. Queen Victoria was a practiced Warrant grantor, handing out more than 2,000 in her sixty-four-year reign, many of which—Fortnum & Mason and R. Twining, for example—are still held today.

A firm must meet certain qualifications to apply for a Royal Warrant, the most significant being that they must have supplied the potential Warrant grantor with their products or services for at least five consecutive years in good standing. The application is then taken under consideration by the royal Household Tradesmen's Warrants Committee. If the application passes muster, they recommend the applicant to the head of the relevant royal household, where a final decision is made by the appropriate royal.

Royal Warrant holders not included elsewhere in this book include:

ASPREY

(Jewelers, Goldsmiths, and Silversmiths)

EST. 1871 ♛ ♛

167 New Bond Street, W1

☎ 020 7493 6767

www.asprey.com

BENTLEY AND SKINNER

(Jewellers and Silversmiths)

EST. 1934 ♛♛

8 New Bond Street, W1

☎ 020 7629 0651

www.bentley-skinner.co.uk

CARLUCCIO'S

(Supplier of Italian Food and Truffles)

EST. 1991 ♛

28 Neal Street, WC1

☎ 020 7240 1487

www.carluccios.com

JUSTERINI AND BROOKS

(Wine Merchants)

EST. 1749 ♛

61 St. James's Street, SW1

☎ 020 7484 6400

www.justerinis.com

MAGGS RARE BOOKS

(Purveyors of Rare Books and Manuscripts)

EST. 1853 ♛

50 Berkeley Square, W1

☏ 020 7493 7160

www.maggs.com

PENHALIGON'S

(Manufacturers of Toilet Requisites)

EST. 1870 ♛

41 Wellington Street, WC2

☏ 020 7836 2150

www.penhaligons.com

RIGBY & PELLER

(Corsetieres)

EST. 1939 ♛

2 Hans Road, SW3

☏ 020 7491 2200

www.rigbyandpeller.com

SMYTHSON OF BOND STREET

(Stationers and Supplier of Leathergoods)

EST. 1887 ♔♔♔

40 New Bond Street, W1

☎ 020 7629 8558

www.smythson.com

SWAINE, ADENEY AND BRIGG

(Whip and Glove Makers and Supplier of Umbrellas)

EST. 1798 ♔♔

54 St. James's Street, SW1

☎ 020 7409 7277

TRUEFITT AND HILL

(Hairdressers)

EST. 1805 ♔

71 St. James's Street, SW1

☎ 020 7493 8496

www.truefillandhill.co.uk

RESTAURANTS, PUBS, AND CAFÉS

Andrew Edmunds

EST. 1964 🦁

46 LEXINGTON STREET, W1

☎ 020 7437 5708   ⊖ OXFORD CIRCUS

MONDAY TO FRIDAY 12:30PM TO 3PM AND 6PM TO 10:45PM;
SATURDAY 1PM TO 3PM AND 6PM TO 10:45PM; SUNDAY 1PM TO
3:30PM AND 6PM TO 10:30PM

FROM THE LOOK AND MENU OF THIS LONG-STANDING SOHO CLASSIC, THE RESTAURANT COULD EASILY BE A hundred years old. Its black-painted shopfront blends seamlessly into the streetscape, making it easy to miss, but its handwritten menu and thoughtful wine list, both posted out front behind a small window, will draw you in. Inside, it's cozy, if cramped. The walls are hung with satirical cartoons from the owners' print gallery next door at number 44 (also worth a visit), and the hodge-podge of tables are topped with fresh flowers. It may look like Dickens' dining room inside, but friendly, lighthanded service and a beautifully composed, simple seasonal menu of—if not strictly British preparations, then smackingly fresh British ingredients—is from another book altogether. The game pie is not to be missed, if on offer. And the wine list, with surprisingly reasonable markups, is always interesting (and French-leaning of late). There is more seating downstairs, but it's darker and less romantic than the ground floor, so those calling for reservations should ask to be seated upstairs.

Bar Italia

EST. 1949

22 FRITH STREET, W1

☎ 020 7437 4520 ⊖ LEICESTER SQUARE

www.baritaliasoho.co.uk

MONDAY TO SATURDAY 24 HOURS; SUNDAY 7AM TO 4AM

IMMORTALIZED IN A CELEBRATED SONG BY PULP, BAR ITAL-
IA'S 1950S FORMICA AND RED LEATHERETTE STOOLS MAY BE
a little faded and worse for wear, but the café is still the undisputed king
of Italian Soho. Fans of the Azzuri flocked here for the 2006 World Cup
(as they do for many Italian club matches; in fact, the television seems
never to cease showing football), spilling out of the tiny space into the
street. It's open 24 hours a day, a rarity for London; the green neon sign
acts a beacon for locals, regulars, and those piling out of the gay clubs,
strip joints, and pubs in the neighborhood after last call.

Bar Italia offers strong coffee (the beans are roasted around the
corner at Angelucci; see page 89), paninis, and pizza. A clutch of outside
tables offers front row seats to the streets of Soho.

Bentley's Oyster Bar and Grill

EST. 1916

11-15 SWALLOW STREET, W1

☎ 020 7734 4756 ⊖ PICCADILLY CIRCUS

MONDAY TO FRIDAY NOON TO 3PM AND 5:30 TO 11PM
(Oyster Bar noon to midnight); SATURDAY NOON TO 3PM AND 5:30
TO 11PM *(Oyster Bar noon to midnight)*; SUNDAY 6PM TO 10PM
(Oyster Bar noon to 10 pm)

THE BACK-ALLEY-LIKE SWALLOW STREET LINKING REGENT STREET TO PICCADILLY SEEMS AN UNLIKELY ADDRESS FOR a posh restaurant; diners are advised to be patient (and perhaps ignore the smell) and look for the giant oyster shell topped by a red neon sign. The Bentley family, who opened the restaurant in 1916, were in the oyster farming business in Suffolk and decided to try their luck in London. At the time, "oyster shops" and "oyster rooms" were gaining popularity as informal places for stop-gap meals—counters at which (usually) men stood and enjoyed freshly shucked shellfish. The Bentleys, however, added a formal dining room and grill to their slightly upscale oyster room, both of which have hosted a regular stream of politicians and theatergoers.

Over time, however, Bentley's lost its sheen and the public's enthusiasm. In 2005, chef Richard Corrigan—who had been head chef under a previous owner—took over, revamped, and inspired a whole new generation of regulars. Prices have gone up, but the food has stayed much the way it was: fresh raw seafood, fish pie, and champagne downstairs; simply prepared game, meat, and fish upstairs in the dining room. The restaurant can seem a tad fussy, and the renovation has stripped the dining room of any historical interest. But the oyster bar is top notch; there is the nonchalant clamor of shucking behind the bar, the service is responsive and cheerful without being cloying, and the seafood takes first place.

E. Pellicci

EST. 1900

332 BETHNAL GREEN ROAD, E2

☏ 020 7739 4873   ⊖ BETHNAL GREEN

MONDAY TO SATURDAY 6:30AM TO 5:00PM; CLOSED SUNDAY

As MODEST AS ANY LONDON "CAFF" AT HEART, PELLICCI'S IS ALSO THE MOST LAVISH. AS LONDON CAFÉ EXPERT Adrian Maddox writes, "See Pellicci's and die."

The first thing you notice is the yellow, enameled glass frontage and chrome lettering. Inside are about ten tables, with elaborate marquetry on the walls and floors. The café was designed in 1946 by Achille Capucci, grandfather of the current owner, Nevio (who was born upstairs). A fire in 2000 destroyed some original detail, but restoration has maintained the lively, decorative spirit of the place.

While all caffs appeal to the broad range of London society, Pellicci's draws one of the most diverse crowds at a greasy-spoon: taxi drivers come in with lists of requests for tea and rolls from their mates at the garage; the artists Gilbert and George are regulars, always cutting a dash in their bespoke suits; all-night party-goers stop in for a full English before going home. The infamous Kray twins were regulars, too.

The high-spirited family still works here every day, and Nevio is never without a tie. On the otherwise uninspiring Bethnal Green Road, Pellicci's is a bright spot, and a true East End landmark.

Franklin's

EST. 1999

157 LORDSHIP LANE, SE22

☎ 020 8299 9598 ⊖ EAST DULWICH RAIL

www.franklinsrestaurant.com

MONDAY TO FRIDAY NOON TO 4PM AND 6PM TO 10PM;
SATURDAY 6PM TO 10:30PM; SUNDAY 6PM TO 10:30PM

CHEF AND OWNER ROD FRANKLIN COMBINES HIS LOVE OF ANTIQUES—HE USED TO RUN AN ANTIQUES BUSINESS IN nearby Camberwell—and food at this South London restaurant. It may seem off the beaten track, but it's only a fifteen-minute trip from London Bridge Station, and worth it for a refreshingly unpretentious room and well-prepared, seasonal food. Oysters are available in season, and Old Spot pork belly, calves liver, and guinea fowl make regular appearances. The exposed brick and lightly decorated walls of the dining room is calming and place all the attention on the food. The classic exterior of the former corner pub is welcoming with its two exposures of windows and constant street bustle. It's a bustling haven for locals, but deserving of the short journey from central London.

Grand Café and Bar

EST. 2002

ROYAL EXCHANGE, THREADNEEDLE STREET, EC3

☎ 0871 0757221   ⊖ BANK

MONDAY TO FRIDAY 8AM TO 11PM;

CLOSED SATURDAY AND SUNDAY

K NOWN PRIMARILY FOR HIS RAILWAY STATIONS AND CEM-
ETERIES, SIR WILLIAM TITE'S 1844 ROYAL EXCHANGE IS
the architect's watershed commission. The commanding location above
Bank tube station is one of London's grandest corners, even if it's often
choked by traffic today. The Exchange has a classical façade that Nikolaus
Pevsner described as marking the decline of the classical revival—sacri-

ficing puritanism for rich decoration. It
is the third Royal Exchange building
on the site; the previous two were both
destroyed by fires (the first in the Great
Fire of 1666). Tite's original interior,
once open to the sky, was covered in 1883,
and stocks and futures ceased being
traded here in 1939; today it is a covered
shopping arcade for luxury goods.

At the very center there is an oval
zinc bar serving simple coffee and crois-

sants in the morning, oysters and prawns at lunch, and champagne in the early evenings. It's a sumptious setting, the zinc reflecting the tile floor and the bustle of the City passing through. Throughout the Exchange (on the weathervane, most notably) there are representations of grasshoppers in homage to the founder of the Royal Exchange, Thomas Gresham, whose family emblem contained a depiction of the Gresham grasshopper.

The portico and exterior courtyard are popular meeting places, with the Bank on one side and Mansion House on the other—and the equestrian statue of the Duke of Wellington presiding over it all.

Holly Bush Pub

EST. 1804

22 HOLLY MOUNT, NW3

☎ 020 7435 2892   ⊖ HAMPSTEAD

www.hollybushpub.com

MONDAY TO SATURDAY NOON TO 11PM;

SUNDAY NOON TO 10:30PM

THE WHITEWASHED HOUSE AT THE BEND OF THIS CUL-DE-SAC WAS USED AS A STABLE FOR SOME NEARBY HOUSES IN the seventeenth century, and possibly as a studio by the society portrait painter George Romney in the late eighteenth century, before being converted into a pub. Gaslights hang from the ceiling of the front room, where a fireplace burns in the autumn and winter; nooks and a "coffee room" (where poetry readings are held on Tuesdays) have been carved out of what used to be Georgian-era living quarters in the back. There's been little change to the furniture and bare oak floors, refreshing in light of the current fashion for over-renovation of old London pubs. Traditional English food is available: a pint of prawns, steak and Guinness pie, and a fine Sunday roast.

J. Sheekey

EST. 1896

28-32 ST. MARTIN'S COURT, WC2

☎ 020 7240 2565 ⊖ COVENT GARDEN

www.j-sheekey.co.uk

MONDAY TO SATURDAY NOON TO 3PM AND 5:30PM TO MID-
NIGHT; SUNDAY NOON TO 3:30PM AND 6PM TO MIDNIGHT

OFF A STREET THAT WAS ONCE A GREAT OPEN DITCH AND WHERE, AFTER THE GREAT FIRE OF 1666, THE WEALTHY began building new homes, sits the mirrored façade of seafood palace J. Sheekey. (Look for the top-hatted doorman in the evenings to locate the entrance.) The restaurant had enough beginnings as an oyster-stall in Shepherd Market owned by Josef Sheekey. In 1896 he expanded his venture in Lord Salisbury's new commercial development in St. Martin's Court in return for providing the Lord with extravagant post-theater dinners.

The restaurant slowly grew in size and its reputation skyrocketed with the success of the nearby West End and with the advent of London's "swinging sixties." But its fortunes waned and the restaurant went bankrupt in 1993. New owners swept in and today it is a discreet haven for the see-and-be-seen, but that doesn't diminish the quality of the seafood, simply prepared. A fish pie and a glass of wine while perched at the busy bar is just as enjoyable as the linen-napkined table service.

Jerusalem Tavern

EST. 1996

55 BRITTON STREET EC1

☎ 020 7490 4281　☻ FARRINGDON

MONDAY TO FRIDAY 11AM TO 11PM;

CLOSED SATURDAY AND SUNDAY

RICHARD HOGARTH (FATHER OF PAINTER WILLIAM HOGARTH) ONCE RAN A TAVERN IN THE RUINS OF THE PRIORY OF ST. John of Jerusalem. Customers were required to speak Latin; it may come as no surprise that it was a short-lived enterprise, no doubt one worthy of his son's satirical wit. Since then, a number of taverns and coffeehouses have taken their name from the priory and existed at nearby Clerkenwell addresses since Britton Street was laid out in 1719. The area was filled with watchmakers, clockmakers, goldsmiths, engravers, and typographers; their window-topped attic workshops (known as "topshops") still crown the curving back streets today.

The current Jerusalem Tavern was originally a merchant's house and later held workshops for watch and clock craftsmen. The frontage visible today with original, now-warped, glass windows dates from 1810, but its charming interior was only created in 1996, when it opened under the name Jerusalem Coffee House. Since then the Suffolk-based St. Peter's Brewery has taken over the pub and has been serving its excellent range of cask ales—one of the few pubs in London to do so. What's not

available on draught is available in St. Peter's unusual green glass bottles, which are based on the quart-sized ale bottles of the eighteenth century (the measurement of which was then known as a "Jerusalem").

Easily located by the clutch of drinkers outside, the tiny tavern serves homemade sausages, cheese plates, and pies at lunchtime. The middle room, where the bar is, has a bird's nest of a balcony with a tiny table for two. There is no more intimate spot to eat and drink on a winter afternoon.

...tyle...
...ng Ale

...ter Ale

...olk Gold

...amon & Apple

...mer Ale

...e Fruit

...y Porter

...den Ale

...m S...

SOUPS · VARIOUS

SPAGHETTI BOLOGNESE
RAVIOLI BOLOGNESE
RISOTTO BOLOGNESE
LIVER · BACON & CHIPS

HAM EGG & CHIPS
ROAST BEEF & VEGETABLES
ESCALOPE · CHIPS & SPAGHETTI
STEAK · EGG & CHIPS
STEAK · CHIPS & SPAGHETTI
MIXED GRILLS & CHIPS
STEAK · CHIPS
LAMB CHOPS · CHIPS
CURRIED BEEF · RICE

SI PARLA ITALIANO

New Piccadilly

EST. 1951

8 DENMAN STREET, W1

☎ 020 7437 8530 ◉ PICCADILLY CIRCUS

MONDAY TO SATURDAY NOON TO 8:30PM; CLOSED SUNDAY

WITHOUT DOUBT THE BEST PRESERVED OF LONDON "CAFFS," THE NEW PICCADILLY MAY BE SLIGHTLY corny (white-jacketed waiters, a neon "EATS" sign in the window) but it is completely authentic. Owned by Pietro Marioni, who emigrated to London after the war, the New Piccadilly was opened in 1951 and is currently managed by the founder's son, Lorenzo. Postcards from loyal customers decorate the walls beside theater posters and red Festival of Britain-era lamps, and it has retained its original fixtures—yellow formica counters, red leatherette booths, Thonet chairs, vintage espresso machine and cash register—and, seemingly, some of its original Soho clientele. It has also kept its 1950s menu, which is printed on a horse-shoe-shaped board and illustrates the hybrid nature of Italian cafés in London: Alongside the usual caff fare of eggs, bacon, and chips, they might offer a decent ravioli or risotto...and chips.

Eel, Pie, and Mash Shops

EEL, PIE, AND MASH SHOPS ARE ONE OF THE GREAT CULI-
NARY TRADITIONS IN LONDON, ESPECIALLY IN THE EAST
End. In the nineteenth century, "pie men" plied the London streets
selling pies made with fish, beef, mutton, and fruit from boxes slung
around their necks. The fish pies sold by some were filled with cooked
eels imported from Holland and brought up the Thames by barges. They
were served with pea soup, mash, and a choice of parsley sauce, chilies, or
vinegar (which is the origin of the accompaniment called "liquor" today),
and they became popular among the poor and working class (especially
in the East End, not far from where the eel barges moored), for their
abundance, cheapness, and healthful qualities. Eels and eel pie became
known as what Frederick Cooke, of the eponymous F. Cooke shops, called
the "poor man's delicacy."

By the 1870s, eel, pie, and mash shops sprang up, which spelled the
end for the pie man. Cooked eels, pie, and mash were served at communal
marble-topped tables or through take-out windows and at street stalls;
live eels for home cooking were sold from barrels outside the shops. By
the middle of the twentieth century there were more than 150 shops.

It's a mystery who invented the dish of jellied (or stewed) eels, and
even today each shop's recipe differs slightly. The way to eat them is to
take an entire piece and chew around the bone in the center. If prepared
correctly, eels should be salty and tender. Jellied eels are served with a
lemon-hued aspic that can be intimidating at first, and is an acquired

texture and taste. But they go down well with a bit of vinegar and spice. Eels are now fished in England and, in a twist of history, exported to Holland. But they are typically served only as a side dish at most pie and mash shops today. Keeping and cooking eels, making pastry, mincing meat, and preparing mash are labor-intensive tasks, and the younger generations at these family-owned businesses are increasingly opting out.

The history of the eel, pie, and mash shop in London is largely the intertwined story of three families: the Cookes, the Manzes, and the Kellys. Tales differ depending on who is asked, as members of some families split off to start their own shops and have a selective memory when it comes to ownership and dates of establishment. The Cookes's first shop was opened in 1862 in Clerkenwell. They opened a shop in Bermondsey in 1891, in the building next door to an Italian family in the ice and ice cream business named Manze, who had emigrated from Ravello. Michele Manze married a Cooke daughter, and opened an eel, pie, and mash shop called Manze's on Tower Bridge Road in 1902. (Today it's owned by their grandson.)

Meanwhile, the Cookes expanded throughout the East End: in Broadway Market near London Fields (1900); in Hoxton (1904); and in Dalston (1910). This last shop, at 41 Kingsland High Street, is now a Chinese restaurant called Shanghai. But it was known as the Buckingham Palace of eel, pie, and mash shops, and the building is Grade-II listed by English Heritage. Its elaborately decorated interior of marble-topped tables, stained-glass skylights, and fine porcelain tiles depicting the Dutch eel barges are well preserved (marble benches and elaborate tiling were common to most eel and pie shops, but sadly few of these

flourishes remain intact in many of them). In its heyday, two tons of live eels were kept in tanks behind the shop.

The Kellys, an Irish family, were latecomers to the eel and pie trade. Their first shop opened in 1958 in the Roman Road, and various family members opened their own shops in nearby Bethnal Green. Today, Kelly's is considered by many to have not only the best eels but the best fruit pies, as well. (The pies at Cooke's, in my opinion, are the best to be had.) Perhaps only twenty-five eel, pie, and mash shops remain, mainly in East and South London. Some worth seeking out for a cheap taste (it's hard to spend more than £5 per person) include:

BJ'S PIE AND MASH SHOP
EST. 1946
330 Barking Road, E13
☎ 020 7174 3389

BERT'S

EST. 1935

3 Peckham Park Road, SE15

☎ 020 7639 4598

F. COOKE

EST. 1900

9 Broadway Market, London Fields, E8

☎ 020 7254 6458

F. COOKE

EST. 1904

150 Hoxton Road, N1

☎ 020 7729 7718

G. KELLY

EST. 1929

414 Bethnal Green Road, E2

☎ 020 7739 3603

G. KELLY

EST. 1938

526-600 Roman Road, E3

☎ 020 8980 3165

GODDARDS

EST. 1933

45 Greenwich Church Street, SE10

☎ 020 8293 9313

HARRINGTON'S

EST. 1923

361 Wandsworth Road, SW8

☎ 020 8672 1877

HARRINGTON'S

EST. 1909

3 Selkirk Road SW17

☎ 020 8672 1877

M. MANZE

EST. 1902

87 Tower Bridge Road, SE1

☎ 020 7407 2985

www.manze.co.uk

M. MANZE

EST. 1927

105 Peckham High Street, SE15

☎ 020 7277 6181

www.manze.co.uk

W. J. ARMENT

EST. 1979

7-9 Westmoreland Road, SE17

☎ 020 7703 4974

Prospect of Whitby

EST. 1543

57 WAPPING WALL, E1

☎ 020 7481 1095 ⊖ WAPPING

MONDAY TO SATURDAY NOON TO 11PM; SUNDAY NOON TO 10PM

THE OLDEST OF THE THAMESIDE TAVERNS, THE PROSPECT OF WHITBY DATES FROM ABOUT 1520. KNOWN THEN AS The Devil's Tavern, much of it was destroyed by fire in the eighteenth century. When it was later rebuilt, it was rechristened the Prospect of Whitby after a ship that moored nearby. The narrow width of the pub is typical of sixteenth-century riverside buildings, but the façade is nineteenth century, as are many of the furnishings inside. Still, it's no less characterful: A long pewter-topped bar sits atop barrels and runs the length of the front room, and the flagstone floor leads off to a windowed dining room overlooking the Thames; beyond that there is an outdoor patio where one can see a hangman's noose, a reminder of the days when the unforgiving "Hanging" Judge Jeffreys frequented the tavern. On a calm weekday afternoon, especially in the autumn and winter with Turneresque skies looming over the river the quiet heart of the Prospect of Whitby feels a million miles from the bustle of London. *(The interesting and often good Wapping Food across the road has generous opening times and is in a splendid space: a former hydraulic station whose power raised and lowered West End theater curtains until the 1970s.)*

Quality Chop House

92-94 FARRINGDON ROAD, EC1

☎ 020 7837 5093   ⊖ FARRINGDON

www.qualitychophouse.co.uk

MONDAY TO FRIDAY 7:30AM TO 10AM AND NOON TO 3PM AND
6:30PM TO 11:30PM; SATURDAY 6PM TO 11:30PM;
SUNDAY NOON TO 10:30PM

FARRINGDON ROAD TRACES THE GHOSTLY LINE THAT WAS THE NEW RIVER—ACTUALLY A CANAL—WHICH BROUGHT fresh water to London. Much of the area was also once marshland owned by St. Paul's Cathedral, which in the mid-1600s was drained and filled

in to establish a new residential district still nominally known as Finsbury, but now mostly referred to as Clerkenwell. The area became known in the nineteenth century for its printers and publishers; few remain, though the offices of the *Guardian* and *Observer* newspapers, which have been in Farringdon Road since the 1960s, are still here. In the 1980s, zoning laws introduced enormous change to the quickly revitalizing neighborhood and have made the area around Exmouth Market,

Clerkenwell Green, and Farringdon Road a popular destination for the many designers and newspaper employees in the area.

The Quality Chop House is in a Grade-II listed building designed by Roland Plumbe, a well-known architect of thoughtfully designed council estates throughout London. It was greatly, but sensitively, refurbished in the mid-1980s. The two dining rooms are slightly cramped but lovely: wooden pew-like booths with etched-glass dividers in the front room; paneled and mirrored walls throughout; original black-and-white diamond tiled floors. It is an exemplar of the nineteenth century workingman's chop house (or "eating house"): restaurants featuring cooking of a caliber a workingman was not likely to get at home, but not considered a luxury. Today it caters less to the "Progressive Working Class" boasted on its etched-glass windows than to the local "meedja" elite, but it still serves traditional British cooking: fishcakes, jellied eels, lambchops, savory pies, grilled liver. Breakfast is also served, including the enormous St. George's: two eggs, a lambchop, bacon, black pudding, mushrooms, tomato, and calve's liver.

Rules

EST. 1798

35 MAIDEN LANE, WC2

☎ 020 7836 5314 ⊖ COVENT GARDEN

www.rules.co.uk

MONDAY TO SATURDAY NOON TO 11:30PM;

SUNDAY NOON TO 10:30PM

NO BOOK ON LONDON'S HISTORIC ESTABLISHMENTS WOULD BE COMPLETE WITHOUT A MENTION OF RULES IN COVENT Garden. Proudly unchanged since it opened in 1798, photos, prints, and clippings cling to every surface such that there's hardly an inch of wall space left uncovered.

Rules began modestly as an oyster bar and was exceedingly popular among writers, actors, and politicians. It is still family owned and run, but no longer by the Rules.

The Italianate building was built in 1873 with a restaurant specifically in mind during the design—unusual for such an early date. The back room has a stained glass skylight that beautifully diffuses the light during the day, and there are three floors of dining rooms. Poet John Betjeman, in his famous crusades to save bits of historic London under threat of redevelopment (see The Blackfriar, page 255), came to the aid of Rules in 1971, when it was at risk of demolition during the rebuilding of Covent Garden market that made it into the glorified mall it is today.

Betjeman called Rules "unique and irreplaceable, and part of literary and theatrical London."

Rules, in a testament to its age and tradition, serves food, in the words of one critic, "as British as the tights Churchill was buried in." While the roasts and steak and kidney pudding certainly fit the bill—and suit most expectations of Britishness—the restaurant specializes in game. Dedicated to responsible sourcing, Rules rears its game on its own estate in the Pennines. Venison and duck are almost always on, and are the highlights of, its menu.

Rules's success is in no doubt due in part to its avoidance of the nouveau cliches of small portions and precious presentation. Diners can come hungry and expect to leave sated; portions are large and the food unaccommodatingly rich. However, Rules is also well served by the constant, nearby tourist trade of Covent Garden and the Opera House, and this is sometimes evident in distracted staff and an overcrowded dining room. Unusual for a restaurant of such repute (and with such high prices), it is open continually throughout the day, so a relaxed late lunch avoids the crowds and focuses the service.

Simpson's Tavern

EST. 1759

BALL COURT, 38½ CORNHILL, EC3

☎ 020 7626 9985   ⊖ BANK

MONDAY TO FRIDAY 11:30AM TO 3PM;

CLOSED SATURDAY, SUNDAY

SIMPSON'S IS IN A WINDING CITY ALLEYWAY OFF CORN-HILL—LOOK FOR THE BOWED WINDOW AND PORTHOLE doors. The building is one of three former "coaching inns" tucked alongside each other; the other two are the George and Vulture pub and the Jamaica Wine House.

Simpson's only serves lunch, takes no bookings, and is closed on weekends. Its menu reads like an English public school dining room fifty years ago: roast beef with freshly grated horseradish, buttery potted shrimps, and steak and kidney pie are all standards, while spotted dick (a steamed dessert pudding—the "spots" are usually currants) is always on offer for dessert. Service is often rushed but never rude. Single diners and small parties may be expected to share a table, but the atmosphere feeds off the lively buzz of regulars.

St. John

26 ST. JOHN STREET, EC1

☎ 020 7251 0848 ⚓ FARRINGDON

www.stjohnrestaurant.co.uk

MONDAY TO FRIDAY 11AM TO 11PM; SATURDAY 6PM TO 11PM;

CLOSED SUNDAY

UNTIL THE MID-NINETEENTH CENTURY, SHEEP AND CATTLE WERE DRIVEN FROM MIDDLESEX AND HERT-fordshire farms down St. John Street and over Cowcross Street to the slaughterhouses at Smithfield Market. So this couldn't be a more appropriate setting for St. John's "nose to tail" eating, in which the delights

of the entire beast—pig's ears to lamb's hearts—are prepared and enjoyed. The establishment is run by Fergus Henderson, a former architect who once cooked at the dining room above The French House (see page 257). The Georgian building has had a colorful past as a smokehouse, a squat, the headquarters of *Marxism Today*, and a warehouse for Chinese beer. Today the undecorated bar and bakery area on the ground floor with a soaring ceiling has a

casual air, while up a small flight of industrial stairs is the more formal dining room.

A favorite—marrow and parsley salad—is always on the menu, a dish that Anthony Bourdain calls, rather bluntly, his "death row meal." Dedicated to responsible husbandry of livestock and the preservation of British traditional ways of eating, none of the animal is put to waste, a practice Henderson describes as "respecting" the animal and the qualities it offers. It's not all flesh and bone, though. The rich Welsh Rarebit is the favorite dish of some, and in season there is a perfectly composed salad of Jerusalem artichokes, roasted red onion, and watercress.

In 2003, a branch—St. John Bread and Wine—opened in Spitalfields (see page 292) serving breakfast and proper elevenses of madeira and seedcake, in addition to lunch and dinner.

Sweetings

EST. 1889

39 QUEEN VICTORIA STREET, EC4

☎ 020 7248 3062   ⊖ MANSION HOUSE

MONDAY TO FRIDAY 11:30AM TO 3PM;

CLOSED SATURDAY AND SUNDAY

A CITY INSTITUTION, SWEETINGS HAS OPERATED ON THIS SITE SINCE 1889 WITH FEW CHANGES IN DECOR, FOOD, or service. Its specialty is simply cooked fish and sublime raw seafood. Its loyal clientele packs its three small rooms at lunchtime (the only time it's open), choosing between a seat at a white linen-covered table or the

mahogany counter for a tray of oysters shucked in front of them, or smoked haddock with poached eggs or fine Welsh Rarebit. Over the din, white-coated waiters—many long in employment here—shout orders and deliver lunch on battered white plates. Traditional puddings such as spotted dick, jam roll, and steamed pudding are on offer, but it's best not to ask for coffee—they don't serve it.

A simple fishmongers when it was originally established, Sweetings has changed hands five times in its history, but the owners all seem to know a good thing: tiled walls, curtained windows, and complete lack of pretension. It is now owned in part by the restaurant's long-time fish supplier, and after nearly 120 years in business has made one concession to modernity: It now accepts credit cards.

The Blackfriar

EST. 1873

174 QUEEN VICTORIA STREET, EC4

☎ 020 7353 6658   ⊖ BLACKFRIARS

MONDAY TO THURSDAY 11:30AM TO 11:00PM; FRIDAY,
SATURDAY 11AM TO 11:30PM; SUNDAY NOON TO 11:30PM

THIS CORNER PUB IS WEDGED UP AGAINST THE RAILWAY LINE AND THE ON-RAMP FOR BLACKFRIARS BRIDGE, A locale neither picturesque nor pleasant, and the quality of the food and beer isn't special either. But it is indispensable for its unique Arts-and-Crafts interior.

Established in the late nineteenth century near the site of a Dominican priory, the pub was rebuilt in 1905 with figures and a frieze by Royal Academy sculptor Henry Poole decorating the exterior. Inside, more of Poole's handiwork can be seen in copper relief narratives of monks' tales amid the garish pink and white-veined marble pillars: There are cheery monks playing flutes, singing, and gathering apples. Lights hang from yokes across the shoulders of monks in relief. The cozy seating area under the arches in the back is no less embellished, as it sits beneath an elaborate mosaic ceiling bearing dogmatic adages such as "Industry is All" and "Wisdom is Rare."

Mirrors, mother-of-pearl inlays, alabaster, stained glass, and marble abound: The lavish decoration was said by architectural historian Andrew

Saint to be a parody of Westminster Cathedral's vaulted interior. It is bizarre but quite wonderful. When it came under threat of demolition in the 1960s, an appeal led by poet John Betjeman rescued it (also see Rules, page 244).

The French House

EST. 1922

49 DEAN STREET, W1

☎ 020 7437 2799   ⊖ TOTTENHAM COURT ROAD

MONDAY TO FRIDAY NOON TO 11PM; SATURDAY NOON TO 11PM;

SUNDAY NOON TO 11PM

"THE FRENCH," AS IT'S CALLED, WAS A FRENCH RESISTANCE HANGOUT DURING THE SECOND WORLD WAR. LATER, ITS regular drinkers included Dylan Thomas and Francis Bacon, who are immortalized in moody photographs plastering the bar's walls. Since then, not much has changed here except the clientele's professions. Nestled in the heart of London's film and theater district, this Soho stalwart attracts actors, film editors, and minor stars of stage and screen. The slightly shabby ground floor bar serves beer only in half pints, and can become wildly crowded. There are a few tables in the back, but if the weather is fair it's more pleasant to rest a glass on the outdoor ledge and watch the Soho crowds go by.

The restaurant upstairs is pretty and comfortable, though the food is unmemorable. It has launched the careers of some great London chefs, though, including Fergus Henderson of St. John (see page 248) and Harvey Cabaniss of Verde (see page 135).

The Grapes

EST. 1720

76 NARROW STREET, E14

☏ 020 7987 4396 ⊖ CANARY WHARF

MONDAY TO FRIDAY NOON TO 11PM;

SATURDAY NOON TO 11PM; SUNDAY NOON TO 10:30PM

SOMETIMES OVERSHADOWED BY ITS OLDER, LARGER UPRIVER NEIGHBOR THE PROSPECT OF WHITBY (SEE P. TK), The Grapes has similar charms: the feel of an old tavern, a riverside location, a terrace overlooking the Thames. It is said that Charles Dickens sang to the customers at The Grapes as a child, and he rechristened it the "Six Jolly Fellowship Porters" in *Our Mutual Friend*.

The ground floor bar and seating area is quite cozy; coziest of all are seats in the back near the fireplace. Upstairs is a well-regarded fish restaurant with a wall of windows overlooking the river. Food is also available downstairs; the gluttonous Sunday roast is a good bet.

This part of the East End was named Limehouse after the lime kilns prevalent in the area in the fourteenth century. Nearby is the Limehouse Cut, linking the Thames and the River Lea. The large early houses along picturesque Narrow Street attest to its high status at the time. Today many of the remaining seventeenth- and eighteenth-century riverside buildings have been expensively restored as private homes, which makes the area no less worthy of a scenic stroll.

The Lamb

EST. 1730

94 LAMB'S CONDUIT STREET, WC1

☎ 020 7405 0713   ⊖ HOLBORN

MONDAY TO SATURDAY 11AM TO 11PM;

SUNDAY NOON TO 4PM AND 7PM TO 10:30PM

THE DELIGHTFULLY NAMED LAMB'S CONDUIT STREET WAS ONCE INDEED A CONDUIT—BUT NOT FOR LAMBS. IT WAS built by philanthropist William Lambe in 1577 to provide the City of London with clean, drinkable water. Today it is a mostly pedestrianized and pleasant diversion from the blandness of central London, full of independent shops and pubs—though a Starbucks has recently moved in despite protests by local residents and shopkeepers. At the north end of the street is Coram's Fields, a park that was the grounds for the

Foundling Hospital in the eighteenth century. It now houses an unusual museum dedicated to the history and mission of the Coram Foundation, which administered the orphanage.

The Lamb is a neighborhood joint, a neighborly place. Pub history devotees rank it

highly for its authentic interior and bar. Founded in the 1720s, it was restored during the Victorian era, and much of what is visible is classic Victorian pub design: etched windows, green fired-brick exterior, and wood walls inside. More unusual, though, are the rarely preserved "snob screens" surrounding the fine U-shaped bar. Patrons could swivel the etched-glass, head-high, pivoting panels to conceal their identity or to obstruct a view of an unappealing drinker. At one time, sections of the bar were probably divided by walls to further the class distinctions between customers. But no longer. Today, the friendly Lamb is abuzz with groups of workers from the nearby hospital, university students, and local residents.

The Scarsdale Tavern

EST. 1885

23A EDWARDES SQUARE, W8

☎ 020 7937 1811　⊖ HIGH STREET KENSINGTON

MONDAY TO SATURDAY NOON TO 11PM;

SUNDAY NOON TO 10:30PM

THE SCARSDALE, SLIGHTLY OFF THE BEATEN PATH IN THE QUIET HOLLAND PARK END OF KENSINGTON, IS A TRUE local pub—even if the locals here are incredibly well-heeled. Its colorfully planted and ivy-covered facade and outdoor tables (heated in the winter—this is Kensington after all) are a respite from the chain stores of the High Street.

Cozy if cluttered, the interior has original moldings along the ceiling, old champagne bottles lining the walls, and a graceful oak bar surrounded by a seating area. There is original signage throughout. It's a shabbily elegant and friendly place.

A stained glass screen divides the bar from restaurant in the back, where full meals are served everyday and where the Sunday roast is said to be particularly good.

The Seven Stars

EST. 1602

53 CAREY STREET, WC2

☎ 020 7242 8521   ⊖ CHANCERY LANE

MONDAY TO FRIDAY 11AM TO 11PM;

SATURDAY, SUNDAY NOON TO 11PM

SITUATED BEHIND THE ROYAL COURTS OF JUSTICE AND HEMMED IN BY CHAIN PUBS, THE SEVEN STARS REMAINS popular with judges and barristers during lunchtimes and on weeknights. But on Saturdays, when all else in the surrounding lanes is closed, it is possible to share the company of the landlady—the boisterous, loveable Roxy Beaujolais—students from nearby King's College and London School of Economics, and other regulars, and enjoy a drink, the newspapers, and some fine food cooked upstairs by Roxy herself. In season there are often oysters, and almost always either homemade sausages, a fine herring and potato salad, and an "elegant BLT" ("deconstructed" might be more accurate). Roxy delightfully describes her food as "refined simplicity without perfectionism."

The pub is one of just a clutch of buildings in the area that survived the Great Fire of 1666. It was originally called The Leg and Seven Stars, a corruption of The League of Seven Stars, a reference to Holland's seven united provinces. Dutch sailors who settled in nearby Ludgate were its early customers, and Benjamin Franklin is said to have lived down the street at number 19 while working as a journeyman printer nearby. Little has been done to the place since then: A clunking dumbwaiter sends the food down to the bar and 2005 saw the sacrifice of the fireplace to make a doorway to some (admittedly, much needed) additional seating. Posters from law-themed films and satirical law prints decorate the walls; lace curtains keep the outside out; and the house cat, Tom Paine, glares from behind his Elizabethan collar if anyone makes a move to share his favorite stool. Customers be warned: Don't try it, even if there isn't an empty seat in the house.

The Wolseley

EST. 1818

160 PICCADILLY, W1

☎ 020 7499 6996 ⊖ GREEN PARK

www.thewolseley.com

MONDAY TO FRIDAY 7AM TO MIDNIGHT;
SATURDAY 9AM TO MIDNIGHT; SUNDAY 9AM TO 11PM

BEFORE THE OUTBREAK OF WORLD WAR I, WOLSELEY MOTORS LIMITED WAS BRITAIN'S LARGEST CAR MAKER, employing 3,000 people and building 4,000 cars a year. By 1921, the company was manufacturing 12,000 cars a year. That year, Wolseley hired architect William Curtis Green to design the most impressive showroom in London. Heavily influenced by Venetian and Florentine architecture, Green's interior had pillars, vaulted celings, starburst marble floors, lacquer and gilt screens, and grand staircases. It was so over the top that architectural critic and historian Nikolaus Pevsner went so far as to call the proportions "irresponsible." It is perhaps no surprise that Wolseley was bankrupt by 1926.

Barclays Bank moved into the building and called in Green to design offices, new furniture, and related objects, including a post box and stamp machine, which can still be seen today. Barclays left the building in 1999, and in 2003 it was transformed into The Wolseley—a European-style grand café and restaurant. There is defintiely something Mittel-

European about the place. The restaurant (where booking is essential) is quite formal, though the service is understated given its grandeur. The café serves food all day in a vaguely louche atmosphere: traditional English breakfasts, salt beef sandwiches, towering *plateau de fruits de mer*, and a good example of the famously difficult-to-get-right Omelette Arnold Bennett, made with haddock, bechamel, and hollandaise sauce. Afternoon tea is also served from 3 pm to 5:30 pm (3:30 pm to 6 pm on the weekend).

Ye Old Mitre

EST. 1546

1 ELY COURT, ELY PLACE, EC1

☏ 020 7405 4751   ⊖ CHANCERY LANE

MONDAY TO FRIDAY 11AM TO 11PM;

CLOSED SATURDAY AND SUNDAY

THIS IS ABOUT AS GOOD AS A LONDON PUB GETS—BUT IS IT REALLY IN LONDON? ORIGINALLY BUILT IN 1546, YE OLDE Mitre sits on land owned and administered by the Bishops of Ely, and so is officially part of Cambridgeshire. It was originally intended to be the watering hole for the servants at the bishops' nearby London home, Ely Palace.

It is a difficult place to find. Visitors should keep an eye out for the bishop's mitre hanging on a lamp post at the curb between two jewelry shops in Hatton Garden, London's diamond district. Down the narrow alley into the pub's courtyard, there is a choice of entering one of two ends of the bar that are not accessible to each other inside the pub, so one must choose carefully. The front area has windows; the back area has a fireplace and a cozy room known as "Ye Closet," where a small party of five or six can fit (snugly). There is a strict edict in place that the furniture not be moved, and one must take care for "ye olde head," as doorways are low and quarters close. Pies and cheese toasties are cheap and come out of the oven quickly.

Fish-and-Chip Shops

GIVEN HOW ICONIC FISH-AND-CHIPS HAS COME TO SEEM OF ENGLISH LIFE, IT IS SURPRISING THAT THE DISH only emerged in the late 1800s. The massive growth of the fish industry in the nineteenth century saw steam trawlers landing fish from all over the North Atlantic, and the rapid expansion of railways meant that fish caught in Aberdeen could be in London within one day.

Though fried fish-and-chips are inseparable today, they evolved distinctly. Fried wedges of potato ("chips"), almost certainly a French invention, became a staple food in the industrial north of England in the nineteenth century. Fried fish, on the other hand, came from the Jewish kitchens of London's East End. One of the earliest recorded fish-and-chip shops in London was Joseph Malin's in Whitechapel, which opened around 1860. But it was in the northern cities that fish-and-chips as a meal in itself first caught on, before spreading to holiday resort towns along the coasts (where it is still a common High Street feature). So essential did fish-and-chips come to be that during the Second World War, the Minister of Food, Lord Woolton, decreed that it would not be rationed. Today there is even a professional body, the National Federation of Fish Friers, which publishes a magazine, the *Fish Friers Review*.

Different types of fish are used in different parts of England, but in London nearly any fish can be found on a chippie menu. Flaky white cod (a specialty of the south of England), hake and haddock (both of them typical of the north of England), and plaice (usually served with its large

271

center bone intact) are the most traditional fish used. A ban on cod from the North Sea has been proposed due to overfishing. Most of the fish used today comes frozen from Norway, Iceland, the Faroe Islands, and Russia. Some recommended fish and chip shops include:

FRYER'S DELIGHT
19 Theobald's Rd, WC1
☎ 020 7405 4114
Taxi drivers' favorite.

GEALE'S
2 Farmer St, London, W8
☎ 020 7727 7528
West London's preferred chippie.

THE GOLDEN HIND
73 Marylebone Lane, W1
☎ 020 7486 3644
Superbly fresh, great chips.

MASTERS SUPER FISH
191 Waterloo Rd, SE1
☎ 020 7928 6924
A good lunch place after a visit to the nearby Imperial War Museum.

ROCK & SOLE PLAICE

47 Endell St, WC2

☎ 020 7836 3785

The oldest fish-and-chip shop in London.

SEA SHELL

49-51 Lisson Grove, NW1

☎ 020 7224 9000

www.seashellrestaurant.co.uk

Near Marylebone, Alfie's Antique Market, and the Lisson Gallery.

TOFF'S

38 Muswell Hill Broadway, N10

☎ 020 8883 8656

Known for being cheerful and family-friendly.

MARKETS

U NTIL WELL INTO THE EIGHTEENTH CENTURY, WHEN LONDONERS WENT OUT FOR GROCERIES OR PROVISIONS they went "marketing" rather than "shopping." As early as 1327, the City of London regulated the market system within the City walls, establishing "Market Rights" that prohibited anyone from setting up a competing market within 6.6 miles of the City—this being the projected distance that a vendor could walk to the market, sell his produce, and return the same day. While some specialist food shops existed, people of all classes relied on the markets for their daily shopping, and a system was in place: Meat was sold on Wednesdays, fish on Fridays. By the Elizabethan Age, London markets began to groan with variety aimed at the gluttonous diets of the growing aristocracy and its increasing taste for the "exotic." The working poor continued to base their diet around bread, cheese, and ale, and only the cheapest cuts of fish and meat were typically available to them. How much a family spent on these "luxuries" offered a clear view of their prosperity.

Regulated or not, chaos reigned: markets spilled over into side streets, and costermongers and barrow boys (street sellers of mainly fruit and vegetables) not sanctioned by the City surreptitiously took advantage of the crowds to unload produce. In the City of London alone twelve retail markets vied for customers until the Great Fire in 1666. Afterward, as the population dispersed, the "suburbs" of the time began boasting more markets of their own as costermongers protested tight City controls. Soon sellers of fruit, meat, live cattle, and fish were given their own, grand covered market halls, while street markets still thrived. Each neighborhood had at least one market day, which became focal points not just for marketing but for social exchange as well. Markets thrived and expanded during the free-spending Victorian era, along with most other versions of consumerism. Thousands of servicemen who returned from World War I without jobs set up as stall holders, increasing their numbers threefold from before the war. In 1936, when László Moholy-Nagy made a series of photographs documenting the life of London street markets, he categorized them as "a social necessity."

Today markets, of course, aren't just for food. Antiques, bric-a-brac, bicycles, and vintage clothes can all be had across London's more well-known covered markets and market streets. While both wholesale and retail markets face increasing competition from chain stores and big box retailers, especially supermarkets, they remain vital in the communities they serve. The role that existing markets play in the lives of many Londoners attests to their place in consumer and cultural history; vendors are often descendants of longtime stall holders.

Many London neighborhoods still have a traditional market street where residents can buy fresh produce and, if they're lucky, meat and fish. But with rage for convenience, the proliferation of large supermarkets, and the fetishization of farmers markets, it's less and less common to find a full-fledged street market that serves a neighborhood constituency on a daily basis. Many of the city's surviving grand market buildings no longer house markets, which have increasingly moved to modern facilities farther from the city center. Still, many are worth a visit for their place in a neighborhood's history, their architecture, and a glimpse at what remains of London's village-like life.

The oldest and grandest of the remaining wholesale markets—Billingsgate for fish and Smithfield for meat—welcome individuals, but a visit requires stamina and an early rise, as they are huge and begin to close up shop before most people have had their first cup of coffee. Individual buyers may also be required to buy in quantity or wait until trade orders have been fulfilled.

Bermondsey Market

EST. 1948

BERMONDSEY SQUARE, TOWER BRIDGE ROAD, SE1

☎ 020 7357 9168 ⊖ BOROUGH

FRIDAY 6AM TO NOON

WHEN NORTH LONDON'S MASSIVE CALEDONIAN MARKET CLOSED DOWN IN THE WAKE OF WORLD WAR II, MARKET traders of antiques, bric-a-brac, and—well—junk, dispersed to other markets across London. Many of the bonafide antiques dealers reassembled in Bermondsey Square, which incorporates the ruins of the eleventh-century Bermondsey Abbey. In recent years, with the archaeological work (revealing the foundations of the church, the remains of which will be preserved and then built over) and the increasing gentrification of this riverside neighborhood near Tower Bridge, the market traders are at risk of being squeezed out to make room for four-star hotels. In the meantime, the market remains robust, if spirits a bit discouraged.

The beauty of Bermondsey Market is that it offers the visitor a kind of tour of Britain's great industries and eras: Endless tables of bone-handled Sheffield plate flatware; piles of coronation china; ivory figurines from various colonial pilgrimages; and fine Victorian and Edwardian jewelry are all to be had in quantity.

Many of the stallholders at Bermondsey are fixtures at Portobello Road or the Wednesday Camden Passage market in Islington, and others have their own shopfronts or deal to the trade. More often than not, they use Bermondsey as a weekly meeting place to sell to each other, hence the early hours, but there are fine items to be found for earlyrisers. Official hours are from 6 am to noon, but, in fact, by 10 or 11 many traders are already beginning to pack up for the day. Visit early, then walk over to Bermondsey Street for breakfast at the Garrison or to Monmouth Coffee in Borough Market (see page 283).

Billingsgate Market

EST. CA. 1400

TRAFALGAR WAY, E14

☎ 020 7987 1118   ⏚ CANARY WHARF DLR

www.cityoflondon.gov.uk/billingsgate

TUESDAY TO FRIDAY 5AM TO 8:30AM;

SATURDAY 5AM TO 8:30AM; CLOSED SUNDAY AND MONDAY

HISTORIANS SAY BILLINGSGATE (KNOWN ALTERNATELY AS BLYNESGATE AND BYLLYNSGATE IN SAXON TIMES) MIGHT refer to a gate in the riverside wall on the southern edge of the City of London where goods were brought ashore, perhaps owned by someone of the name "Boling" or "Biling." A thousand-year-old inventory of London establishments— "Ethelred's Institutes of London"—makes mention of it as a market, most likely for coal, iron, wine, salt, and pottery, but it wasn't until the sixteenth century that Billingsgate was known for specializing in fish. This role was made official by an Act of Parliament in 1699, which declared it "a free and open market for all sorts of fish," with the exception of eels (see page 235), which were the domain of the Dutch fishermen who barged up the Thames and through the canals selling eels to pie men. These fishermen were granted the privilege of selling outside the confines of the market system, as they had helped feed victims of the Great Fire in 1666.

By the nineteenth century, the amount of business fishermen were conducting and the haphazard proliferation of stalls around the docks demanded that some order be instilled. While there is evidence of some kind of pavilion-like structure from as early as 1598, a permanent market hall was finally built for fishmongers in 1850, on Lower Thames Street along the river between the Monument and the Customs House. But it was deemed inadequate and demolished less than twenty-five years later to make way for a new yellow-brick building designed by City of London architect Horace Jones. Fish stalls lined the short sides and shellfish were sold in the basement, and strangely inappropriate sea-themed decorations (dolphins?) cover the roof level, where the architect hoped to house a pub or two. The building remained in use as London's main fish market until 1982; in the late 1990s it was converted into offices by architect Richard Rogers.

The new fish market, still called Billingsgate, was moved to Poplar, in the shadow of Canary Wharf. One of the first buildings to open after the controversial closing of the docks in 1980, the structure is a conversion and extension of a depot shed used by Transport for London, topped by bright yellow steel tubes. It sits marooned among the last vestiges of an industrial landscape, and increasingly surrounded by shiny new financial industry skyscrapers. Today it is the largest market in the UK (covering thirteen acres) and trades around 25,000 tons of fish a year (a surprising 40% of it imported). Visitors are advised to arrive early and wear a pair of sturdy, nonslip shoes.

Borough Market

EST. 1756

8 SOUTHWARK STREET, SE1

☎ 020 7407 1002   ◎ LONDON BRIDGE

FRIDAY NOON TO 6PM; SATURDAY 9AM TO 4PM;

CLOSED SUNDAY

WHILE BOROUGH MARKET IS ONE OF LONDON'S OLDEST PRODUCE MARKETS, TODAY IT IS BY FAR THE MOST famous food market in Britain. A busy Saturday under the railroad bridges and beneath the arches will find tourists, locals, restaurant chefs, and television crews vying for the best views of immaculately displayed

homegrown and imported food. Friday afternoons were once a near private shopping experience, with local office workers lining up for Brindisa's chorizo sandwiches or the great falafel at the stall toward the front of the market. But the ever-growing popularity of Borough Market and the recent restoration and growth of the Saturday market has meant that Friday is no less hectic than the weekend. The market hasn't quite outgrown its reputation yet, but Borough teeters on the edge of being almost too big and unwieldy, which is to say, far too tempting, as well as occasionally frustrating. Visitors will not leave empty handed (or empty of stomach). Go for farmhouse cheeses sold by the producer, cascading displays of just-caught seafood, homemade jams and chutneys, the most beautiful produce displays this side of rue Daguerre, and expect to feel the most incredible urge to cook with the best ingredients.

The Romans built the first of many "London Bridges" spanning the Thames in AD43, and the Borough Market has been trading ever since either on the bridge or just at its south side, as it is today. In Roman times, the market more likely specialized in fish and meat than produce. It wasn't a formally recognized institution until 1276, and has been operating continually as a wholesale fruit and vegetable market in its present location since 1756. Produce from all over the British Empire would arrive by boat at the nearby docks, which became know as "London's Larder" for the sheer quantity of food that passed through.

Columbia Road Market

EST. CA. 1850

COLUMBIA ROAD, E2

☎ 020 7377 8963   ⊖ LIVERPOOL STREET

SUNDAY 8AM TO 2PM

DURING THE WEEK, THE COLORFUL, SHUTTERED SHOP-FRONTS AND SLEEPY ATMOSPHERE OF COLUMBIA ROAD have an almost Parisian feel. The newsagent, the baker, the pub, and the modest tapas restaurant account for any buzz to be had; during the school year, from behind the high walls of the local primary school the pleasant din of kids playing at recess can be heard. But on Sundays, the neighborhood transforms completely. It seems as if all of London (and much of Essex) has converged on the two or three sardine-packed blocks that host the Columbia Road Flower Market for cut flowers and bedding plants, not to mention organic coffee, cupcakes, and olive oil.

By London standards, Columbia Road is a relatively young market. In the mid 1800s, flower and produce sellers set up every weekend in one block of the road, just slightly to the west of where the market takes place today, plying their wares to the area's broad population of the working poor, the moderately successful furniture makers and upholsterers, and some well-off business owners.

Around the same time, Charles Booth was embarking on his meticulous door-to-door socio economic survey of London, which resulted in the fascinating and beautifully rendered Booth Poverty Maps (on view at the Museum of the City of London). Fresh philanthropic attention was being paid to the area, one of the poorest in East London, and the conditions that many were working and living in, resulting in the building of the nearby Boundary Estate and Leopold Buildings (visible from the market at the corner of Columbia and Hackney Roads). One of the most active philanthropists in the area was the Baroness Burdett-Coutts, who provided the funding to build a market hall for the traders that opened in 1869 (her other charitable efforts ranged from creating a sewing school for girls in Spitalfields to installing drinking fountains for dogs). The grand gothic revival folly was enormous—and was built for the enormous sum of £200,000—but proved just that, a folly. The street venders believed that the market hall was an attempt to clear them from the streets so in protest they simply continued to set up their stalls in the street. The hall closed in 1874, remained unused, and was, regrettably, torn down in 1958. All that remains of the old market is the tiny bit of iron and stone gate fronting the nursery school on Columbia Road.

Today, in addition to the plants and cut flowers offered from the street stalls, the decidedly upscale Columbia Market now encompasses the shops lining the roads and two courtyard markets that sell garden furniture, pottery, antiques, food, furniture, and books. Not to be missed are Angela Flanders' perfumerie (No. 96), Fred Bare Hats (No. 118), Jones Dairy (see page 127), Treacle (No. 160), and the beautiful interior of the Royal Oak pub (No. 73), which offers good food in the bar or in the informal dining room upstairs.

Leadenhall Market

EST. 1881

GRACECHURCH STREET, EC1

☎ 020 7332 3099   ⊖ BANK

DAILY 8AM TO 6PM (PUBS AND RESTAURANTS LATER);

SATURDAY 10AM TO 5PM; CLOSED SUNDAY

THE CATHEDRAL PROPORTIONS OF THE LEADENHALL MARKET ARE SOMEWHAT APPROPRIATE—IN THE SECOND century, the basilica of a Roman forum stood on the site. Records of a market here go back as far as 1321, when it was held in the courtyard of the mansion named "Le Leden Halle." In 1345, Leadenhall became the designated poultry market for mongers from outside the City (those poultry dealers who were London citizens sold their goods in nearby Poultry, a street that still exists, about five minutes away). In 1881 the present building by Horace Jones, architect of the (original) Billingsgate and Smithfield Markets, was erected and the design modeled on a medieval street layout, resulting in long intersecting aisles of open stalls with offices along a mezzanine above. When health and hygiene laws changed in the 1970s, most of the storefronts were glazed and, after a restoration in the early 1990s, became home to a series of predictable chain boutiques and popular after-work pubs. A bit of history remains in the sympathetic restoration, however. Meat hooks and rails were never removed and an old-fashioned, family fishmonger remains at the Gracechurch entrance:

HS Linwood and Son, who has had a stall here since 1980s and sets out a wonderful fish display in its (still) open-fronted stall. On Fridays, a fine food market sets up in the center. Also in the market is The Lamb Tavern, which contains an excellent tiled illustration called "Building the Monument: 1671 Christopher Wren Explaining his Plans"—a little bit of local history with your pint!

Portobello Road Market

EST. CA. 1870

PORTOBELLO ROAD, W11

☎ 020 7229 8354   ⊖ NOTTING HILL GATE

www.portobelloroad.co.uk

SATURDAY 8:00AM TO 6PM

P ORTOBELLO ROAD WAS ONCE A LANE LEADING TO PORTO-
BELLO FARM, WHICH WAS NAMED AFTER PUERTO BELLO,
the Panamanian city captured in 1739 by Admiral Edward Vernon in a
colonizing conflict known as "The War of Jenkin's Ear." Today Portobello
Road is a vein running through the heart of Notting Hill, famous for its
massively popular Saturday antiques market with 700 stalls, including a
group of them named for Admiral Vernon. The street has held a daily
market—for produce, bric-a-brac, and household goods—since the late
nineteenth century, when the area was virtually a village on the edge of
urbanizing West London.

This is London's preeminent antiques market. Dealers offer everything from old leather footballs and cricket bats to fine jewelry and
vintage clothing, while tourists and locals navigate the traffic and gawk.
In 1923, the MP William Bull wrote of Portobello Road market that "on
Saturdays in the winter...the people overflowed from the pavements so
that the roadway was quite impassable for horse-traffic. On the east side
were costers' barrows, lighted by flaming naphtha lamps. In the side

streets were side-shows." Aside from the horses, not much has changed: On Saturdays it is still among the busiest streets in the city.

The movie *Notting Hill* popularized the area to the breaking point, and gentrification has made it one of the most expensive in London. But Notting Hill has a deep history of racial and class tension and poor postwar planning decisions that can hardly be missed as you walk down Portobello Road. Long a community of large middle class households, Notting Hill's grand homes lost appeal and value during the interwar years and developers split up houses into shabby SROs; by the 1940s much of the area was a slum. Notting Hill in decline became the backdrop for the novels of G.K. Chesterton, the Ann Jellicoe play *The Knack (and How to Get It)* and Horace Ove's 1974 film *Pressure*. Newly arrived immigrants from the West Indies who settled in the area were charged exorbitant rents for negligible conditions and population density was among the highest in London. During the summer of 1958 gangs of white locals assaulted their new neighbors. Racial tensions continued when Oswald Mosley—onetime leader of the British Union of Fascists and husband of Diana Mitford—returned to London briefly from a self-imposed exile and ran for the MP spot in nearby North Kensington. (He lost, but disputed the count.)

In the mid-1960s, the elevated M40 highway, known as the Westway, sheared through the northern end of Notting Hill, levelling homes, erasing streets, and exposing those who weren't displaced to the constant thrum and light of a major highway going past their homes. Beginning in the 1980s, Notting Hill's large houses again became attractive to those willing and able to take on massive restoration projects that set the neighborhood on the road to a sort of recovery and the renaissance it's been experiencing of late. Despite its fractured history and rapid gentrification, Notting Hill remains a diverse part of London that is worth exploring quite apart from market day.

While on Portobello Road, there are a couple of independent shops worth seeking out: Honest Jon's Records (No. 276) is an independent jazz, soul, and reggae record label and shop that has released, among other titles, the incomparable compilation series *London Is the Place for Me*, a virtual soundtrack chronicling the African and Caribbean immigration to London. The Cloth Shop (at No. 290) specializes in antique French table linens and ticking, Irish linen, Welsh blankets, and English wools. Jars and boxes of antique buttons decorate the front shelves of the shop and seem to be for sale only at the owner's whim.

Spitalfields Market

EST. 1887

COMMERCIAL STREET, E1

☎ 0207 247 8556   ⊖ LIVERPOOL STREET

www.spitalfields.org.uk

SUNDAY 9AM TO 5PM; CLOSED SATURDAY

FOR HUNDREDS OF YEARS, SPITALFIELDS (NAMED FOR THE OPEN SPACE THAT ONCE EXISTED AROUND THE THIRTEENTH-century St. Mary's Hospital has been a gateway for waves of new immigrants and exiles. In the late 1600s, persecuted Huguenot weavers fled France, set up in the area, and helped establish the robust weaving and textile trade that flourished until the nineteenth century, when German refugees arrived just as the area was beginning to fall on hard times and factories took the place of handmade silks. Eastern European Jews flowed into Spitalfields in the late nineteenth century, and the area was as overcrowded and destitute as any in London, when the clothing trade, a large brewery, and tobacco warehouses employed many local residents under horrendous working conditions. The next wave of immigration, mainly from Bangladesh, reached its height in the 1970s. As a testament to the area's history of immigration, one need only look at the local mosque on Brick Lane, which successively housed a Huguenot chapel, a Methodist church, and a synagogue—before becoming a masjid in 1975. Today Spitalfields and nearby Brick Lane are a complex, and not always complementary, mix of artists and designers, Bangladeshi restaurant workers, and those privileged enough to restore and occupy some of the finest eighteenth-century residential architecture in London.

The heart of it all is the bustling Spitalfields Market. In 1682, King Charles granted a license for "flesh, fowl, and roots" to be sold on the site, and it has held some semblance of a market ever since. Today banners proclaim: "Open. Since 1887." Indeed, market organizers and preservationists have reason to boast of its longevity. Entirely rebuilt between 1883 and 1893, it was East London's main fruit and vegetable market and operated until 1986. In the mid-1990s, near-unchecked development forced the demolition of two-thirds of the historic market hall. A series of banal, glass, Norman Foster-designed office buildings hugs the western side of the market in its place, albeit creating two much-needed public spaces quite popular with local office workers.

The eclectic Sunday market that occurs today has been open since 1993. It is the major attraction in Spitalfields, and coupled with Brick Lane's "Sunday UpMarket," draws about 15,000 people every week. Fruits and vegetables are still sold on a modest scale at the weekend, and a new Thursday/Friday/Sunday fine food market sees local businesses and London foodie favorites setting up stalls. On Thursdays, antique dealers set up their tables. Echoing its past as a garment and fabric center, in recent years Spitalfields has become a central stage for young talent from the fashion colleges to sell their designs directly to consumers.

ACKNOWLEDGEMENTS

I would like to thank Angela Hederman, Celine Keating, and Louise Fili Ltd. for their support, editing, and design of this book, respectively. I am grateful for the assistance (and patience) of the staffs at the Guildhall Library and the London Library. Phil Nicholls' adoration for and appreciation of traditional London resulted in the thoughtful and evocative images throughout the book.

Matt Weiland's comments and companionship, as ever, made it better.

BIBLIOGRAPHY

Ackroyd, Peter. *London: The Biography* (London: Vintage, 2001)

Adams, Tim, ed. *City Secrets London* (New York: The Little Bookroom, 2001)

Adburgham, Alison. *Shops and Shopping, 1800-1914* (London: George Allen and Unwin, 1981)

Benson, John and Laura Ugolini, eds. *A Nation of Shopkeepers: Five Centuries of British Retailing* (London: IB Tauris, 2003)

Davis, Dorothy. *History of Shopping* (London: Routledge, 1966)

Driver, Christopher. *The British at Table* (London: Chatto & Windus, 1983)

Glinert, Ed. *The London Compendium: A Street-by-Street Exploration of the Hidden Metropolis* (London: Penguin, 2004)

Haydon, Peter. *The English Pub: A History* (London: Robert Hale, 1994)

Heathcoate, Edwin. *London Caffs* (London: Wiley-Academy, 2004)

Henderson, Fergus. *Nose to Tail Eating: A Kind of British Cooking* (London: Macmillan, 1999)

Inwood, Stephen. *City of Cities: The Birth of Modern London* (London: Macmillan, 2005)

Linford, Jenny. *Food-Lovers' London* (London: Metro Publications, 2005)

Ehrman, Edwina, Forsyth, Hazel, et al. *London Eats Out. 500 Years of Capital Dining* (London: Philip Wilson Publishers, 1999)

Maddox, Adrian. *Classic Cafes* (London: Black Dog Publishing, 2003)

Morrison, Kathryn A. *English Shops and Shopping: An Architectural History* (London: Yale University Press, 2003)

Orwell, George. *Essays* (New York: Everyman's Library, 2002)

Pevsner, Nikolaus, et al. *The Buildings of London, Volumes 1-6* (London: Yale University Press, 2002)

Porter, Roy. *London: A Social History* (London: Penguin, 1994)

Venables, Sally, with Williams, Steve. *Still Open: The Guide to Traditional London Shops* (London: Black Dog Publishing, 2006)

INDEX

INDEX BY AREA OF LONDON

ABOUT THE AUTHOR

Eugenia Bell is a freelance writer and editor of books on art, architecture, design, and travel. She has written for *Artforum*, *ID*, *frieze*, and *Lingua Franca*. She is the author of *The Civilized Traveller's Guide to Turin*, published by The Little Bookroom. After living in London for several years, she recently moved back to New York.

ABOUT THE PHOTOGRAPHER

Phil Nicholls has been a photographer for more than twenty years, working mainly in the music industry. He is currently working on a long term project documenting the River Thames. He is the photographer of the book *Classic Cafes*, written by Adrian Maddox (Black Dog Publishing, 2003).